PRESERVING LOS ANGELES

HOW HISTORIC PLACES CAN TRANSFORM AMERICA'S CITIES

REHABILITATION IN THE BROADWAY HISTORIC COMMERCIAL AND THEATER DISTRICT HAS BEEN A CATALYST FOR DOWNTOWN L.A.'S ECONOMIC REVITALIZATION.

PRESERVING LOS ANGELES

HOW HISTORIC PLACES CAN TRANSFORM AMERICA'S CITIES

KEN BERNSTEIN

PHOTOGRAPHY BY STEPHEN SCHAFER

ACP
ANGEL CITY PRESS

EARLY TWENTIETH-CENTURY CRAFTSMAN BUNGALOWS IN THE JEFFERSON PARK HISTORIC PRESERVATION OVERLAY ZONE (HPOZ).

CONTENTS

LOS ANGELES
FROM BEHIND THE
HOLLYWOOD SIGN.

INTRODUCTION
HISTORIC PRESERVATION?
IN LOS ANGELES?

MISUNDERSTANDING LOS ANGELES

In the public imagination, the name "Los Angeles" conjures images that tend to fall within two extremes. The first is a land of Tinseltown glamour and Hollywood celebrities, with sunshine, beaches, and palm trees. The other is a dystopia punctuated by ugly sprawl, soul-crushing traffic, and cultural vapidity.

Both of these images feed into a common trope, prevalent among outside observers and Angelenos alike: that Los Angeles is a city that's never cared much about its history or its historic buildings. Sometimes, L.A. is described more tactfully as a city that has a "complicated relationship" with its past.

To be sure, such assertions are not completely without substance. Los Angeles is a younger city than many of its East Coast or European counterparts. Its post-World War II explosion in freeways and suburban development, as well as its traditional openness to creativity and new ideas, have also given the city a perennial image as the City of the Future. But that's not the whole story, either.

DOWNTOWN'S INDUSTRIAL DISTRICT IS AN ANCHOR OF THE NATION'S LARGEST MANUFACTURING CENTER.

THE REAL LOS ANGELES: CONTRADICTIONS AND MULTITUDES

The real Los Angeles is something quite different than these simplistic assumptions. It is a richly complex city: large, containing multitudes, with seemingly baffling contradictions.

Assertions about Los Angeles's comparatively short history generally fail to acknowledge that, for thousands of years, indigenous communities that included the Fernandeño Tataviam, the Gabrielino/Tongva/Kizh, and the Ventureño Chumash made today's Los Angeles their home.

While it may be younger than many other American cities, Los Angeles has a remarkable collection of architectural resources in all styles, reflecting the legacy of notable designers from the past 150 years. Los Angeles's built environment features one of the nation's most diverse mixes of building types. The city does have its share of sprawling single-family tracts, but it also has intensely urbanized centers such as Downtown and Hollywood. Its built form ranges across early suburbs of historic homes from the late nineteenth and early twentieth centuries, 1920s and 1930s multi-family neighborhoods, linear commercial corridors, hillside mini-towns, and even equestrian and semi-rural neighborhoods.

Overall, the real Los Angeles is actually a remarkably dense city. According to the U.S. Census Bureau, the Los Angeles-Long Beach-Anaheim region is the most densely populated urbanized area in the United States—even more dense than the overall New York region.

Los Angeles is one of the most diverse cities in the world, with residents reflecting the entire international community, speaking over one hundred languages. Only a small percentage of Los Angeles residents have anything to do with Hollywood's glamour; more than 95

THE VERMONT KNOLLS NEIGHBORHOOD IN SOUTH LOS ANGELES, IDENTIFIED AS A SIGNIFICANT HISTORIC DISTRICT IN SURVEYLA.

percent of Los Angeles residents do not work in "The Business" (entertainment), which is only one of many industries that define the city. Even today, according to the U.S. Bureau of Labor Statistics, the Los Angeles region remains the largest manufacturing center and workforce of any region in the country, building upon an industrial legacy that includes aerospace, food, oil, and many other enterprises.

And Los Angeles does have an energetic and engaged constituency that is passionate about the city's history and preserving significant historic places. The non-profit Los Angeles Conservancy, formed in 1978 around the fight to save the Los Angeles Central Library from demolition, grew within two decades to have the largest membership of any local non-profit historic preservation organization in the country.

PRESERVATION IN A CHANGING CITY

Like all large cities, Los Angeles continues to change rapidly. The continuing challenges of growth and a deepening housing crisis have led to ongoing real estate development pressures and high land prices that generate continual new threats to existing buildings, heightening the peril for those buildings and other places that have long anchored local communities.

How does a dynamic city like Los Angeles sort out what is worth preserving as it continues to grapple with rapid change? How can preservation lead a city forward to absorb change without losing its past?

Many critics of historic preservation argue that historic preservation protections by their very nature stifle change and dynamism in cities. In a 2019 critique of historic designations in *Forbes* magazine, Adam Millsap writes, ". . . Entire neighborhoods of marginal historical value are frozen in time, hindering the ability of cities

and their residents to adjust their built environments in response to changing economic circumstances . . . Widespread historic designations impede adaptation and may result in a city's past determining its future." But Millsap's assertions are a crude caricature of historic preservation.

Historic preservation at its best is not about stopping change or freezing buildings or places in time—it's our best method of managing change. Preservation actually can be an engine of positive change, driving the evolution or adaptation of existing buildings, or even significant additions, to better accommodate the needs of new users and the demands of current ways of life.

Most of the most positive adaptations and changes defining today's Los Angeles have been driven by, not hindered by, historic designations and rehabilitation. Neighborhoods and buildings that have been a focus of preservation activity often contrast starkly (and positively) with those areas that have remained free of thoughtful "change management." The most popular and vital places in Los Angeles—those areas with the most active real estate development markets—are increasingly areas that have the highest concentrations of historic buildings. Homebuyers, residential tenants, and commercial businesses alike are seeking out the beauty and authenticity that only historic spaces can provide.

Preserving the Past, Transforming the Future

All across the city, historic preservation activity has been transforming Los Angeles, while also pointing the way to how other cities can use preservation to revitalize their own neighborhoods and build community.

The book's focus is on the City of Los Angeles—rather than the much larger Los Angeles/Orange County region—in part because the City of Los Angeles is a region unto itself, with approximately 470 square miles. While more than two-thirds of the eighty-eight cities in Los Angeles County have no local historic preservation laws at all, the City of Los Angeles has developed one of the most successful local historic preservation programs in the U.S. The city's accomplishments have included the completion of the nation's largest and most ambitious citywide survey of historic resources, identifying cherished places in every Los Angeles neighborhood.

The L.A. preservation story starts with the city's designated local landmarks, or City Historic-Cultural Monuments. Los Angeles was a national pioneer among major cities in establishing a local program to designate historic landmarks in the early 1960s. By designating significant landmarks, Los Angeles has been preserving—and sometimes rescuing at the eleventh hour—many more cherished places than it is losing to rampant real estate pressures.

In addition to these separately designated historic sites, L.A. is truly a city of neighborhoods, with remarkable, cohesive groupings of historic buildings, often just off the city's major boulevards but well off the beaten path for tourists. Today, Los Angeles has the nation's second-largest program to preserve local historic districts (called Historic Preservation Overlay Zones, or HPOZs, in L.A.). These HPOZs are creating significant economic value and a sense of community in their historic neighborhoods, as described in Chapter 2.

Every community in the city has architectural treasures and cherished places, often ignored or hidden in plain sight. To identify these places, the City of Los Angeles has completed SurveyLA, its first-ever citywide survey of historic resources, through a unique and productive partnership with the J. Paul Getty Trust, described in Chapter 3. SurveyLA Discoveries at the end of the book highlights dozens of the most interesting finds from the survey—lesser-known buildings, neighborhoods, and places in every corner of the city that have been identified and are now informing planning initiatives to shape the future of these neighborhoods.

Los Angeles has also been extending historic preservation beyond its traditional focus on the preservation of significant architecture, to identify and protect the places that have cultural significance or social meaning to all of Los Angeles's diverse communities. The Office of Historic Resources has been creating preservation frameworks, highlighted in Chapter 4, to ensure that the L.A. story more fully reflects the legacies and places associated with L.A's rich ethnic diversity and cultural history.

Preservation in Los Angeles has led the way in creating a Downtown renaissance, fueled by the power of "adaptive reuse": converting older buildings to newer purposes. The conversion of historic commercial and industrial buildings to new housing units Downtown, facilitated by the city's Adaptive Reuse Ordinance, has proven to be the single most significant factor in transforming Los Angeles's urban core as discussed in Chapter 5.

In more recent years, the impacts of adaptive reuse and creative rehabilitation have begun spreading to all corners of the city. Rehabilitation projects are increasingly creating affordable housing, centers of community, and neighborhood anchors. Developers and property owners are finding that preservation and adaptive reuse add economic value to their projects, as Angelenos increasingly seek out buildings with history, beauty, and authenticity as their preferred places to live and work.

Historic preservation is making a difference not only in prominent places like Downtown Los Angeles and Hollywood, but in communities throughout the city:

from Canoga Park in the West San Fernando Valley to the Harbor community of Wilmington; from the Westside neighborhood of Mar Vista to the late-nineteenth century original streetcar suburb of Lincoln Heights, northeast of Downtown.

JOURNEYING THROUGH HISTORIC LOS ANGELES

Those visiting Los Angeles for just a few days often find many of their preconceptions confirmed, as they stick to typical tourist destinations such as Disneyland, Universal Studios, or Hollywood Boulevard. The city's sheer size makes it difficult for the casual visitor to take in the totality of L.A., or to understand it in any meaningful way.

Preserving Los Angeles, while not a guidebook per se, offers a very different kind of journey through Los Angeles, stopping at places of beauty and significance that even most longtime Angelenos don't know. Along the way, "Preservation Profiles" highlight some of the people whose passion and energy have helped make these changes possible.

Preserving Los Angeles showcases every community within the Los Angeles city limits, since every community has sites with remarkable architecture or cultural meaning. For a Los Angeles resident, that means finding some hidden gems to explore. And for out-of-towners, these discoveries will help locate not only the real Los Angeles, but also a pathway toward understanding how historic preservation can transform any community.

THE GARDEN OF OZ IN THE HOLLYWOOD HILLS, HISTORIC-CULTURAL MONUMENT #996

LOS ANGELES CITY
HALL, LOS ANGELES
HISTORIC-CULTURAL
MONUMENT #150

CHAPTER 1
RESCUING LANDMARKS:
LOS ANGELES'S HISTORIC-CULTURAL MONUMENTS

LOS ANGELES:
A PRESERVATION PIONEER

One of the basic building blocks of any local historic preservation program is a local ordinance, or law, that allows for the designation of historic landmarks. This allows a municipality to choose the buildings and places that are most cherished within the community and confer some level of protection against demolition or major changes.

Given L.A.'s image as a city of perennial change, many are surprised to learn that the City of Los Angeles passed one of the earliest municipal landmark laws in the nation. With its Cultural Heritage Ordinance of 1962, Los Angeles took action years before similar local preservation laws were passed in New York (1965), San Francisco (1967), San Diego (1967), Chicago (1968), Boston (1975), and most other major U.S. cities.

Since then, Los Angeles has designated over 1,200 buildings, sites, and natural features as Historic-Cultural Monuments (HCMs), or local landmarks. HCM designation has resulted in the recognition of significant sites of Los Angeles architecture and history, and has led to numerous dramatic rescues and remarkable transformations of historic places—from threatened residential complexes to iconic commercial buildings, and from architectural oddities to sites of civic importance or deep social and cultural meaning.

Despite these distinctions and successes, most accounts of Los Angeles's contemporary history have overlooked the key role that official historic designation has played in saving or revitalizing key historic places. And few Angelenos have an understanding of how the places they cherish might become a designated landmark.

CREATING A LANDMARKS PROGRAM

In many cities, high-profile demolition threats or widespread destruction have triggered preservation action. In Los Angeles, a small group of members within the city's chapter of the American Institute of Architects (AIA) became alarmed in 1958 by the destruction of historic buildings in Downtown and other neighborhoods, created by the explosion of growth in post-World War II Los Angeles. The AIA Historic Building Committee and L.A.'s Municipal Art Commission proposed a local ordinance to identify and protect historic sites throughout the city.

The 1962 Cultural Heritage Ordinance created a five-member, mayoral-appointed citizen board, the Cultural Heritage Board, with the authority to designate as Historic-Cultural Monuments any building, structure, or site important to the history of Los Angeles, the state, and the nation.

The year 1962 was a time of significant change in Los Angeles, with the strong post-war economy continuing to fuel rapid growth and development. Just the year before, the last of the Pacific Electric Red Car trolleys, running between Los Angeles and Long Beach, had ceased operations, signaling the final victory of the automobile in a once-transit-oriented metropolis. This was the era of "urban renewal" across the nation, supported by the federal government and implemented by local governments, based on the premise that "slums" needed to be "cleared" through wholesale demolition and new construction. Los Angeles's major urban renewal project, the redevelopment of Downtown's Victorian-era neighborhood, Bunker Hill, was getting into full swing in 1962. And that year, another previous example of "slum clearance"—the expulsion of longtime residents from Chavez Ravine—culminated in the opening of Dodger Stadium, which was viewed as a symbol of modernity and L.A.'s new "major league" status, despite the significant human cost associated with its development.

Amidst this Los Angeles of rapid change and modernity, a new Cultural Heritage Board stepped forward with a mandate to protect the most important places of L.A.'s history. William Woollett, FAIA, who had led the AIA's Historic Buildings Committee, was elected as the first president of the Cultural Heritage Board. Carl Dentzel, the longtime director of the Southwest Museum, was an original board member and remained on

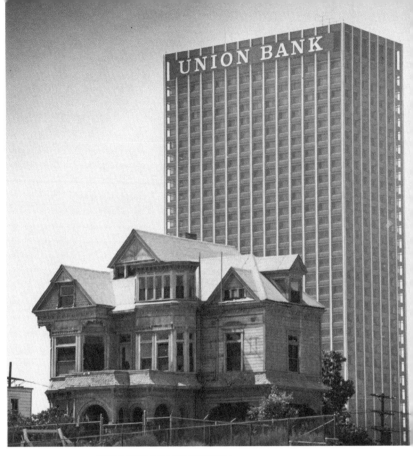

THE CASTLE ON BUNKER HILL,
IN THE SHADOW OF THE NEW UNION BANK TOWER,
PREPARED FOR RELOCATION TO HERITAGE SQUARE, 1966-68.

the board until 1980. Prominent architectural historian and author Robert Winter also served on the board from 1972 to 1984.

At the board's first meeting, on August 6, 1962, it boldly declared five sites as Historic-Cultural Monuments, all of which were under threat at the time. The Leonis Adobe (1844), the former residence of rancho owner and sheep herder Miguel Leonis and his Chumash Indian wife, Espiritu Chijulla, located on Los Angeles's border with Calabasas, was under immediate threat of demolition. The board's designation resulted in a stop work order and the home's ultimate preservation; the adobe has the honor of being designated as Historic-Cultural Monument #1. Bolton Hall in Tujunga, the

Plaza Church at El Pueblo, Angels Flight Railway, and the Salt Box mansion on Bunker Hill (later destroyed by fire) were also designated at the first meeting.

WHAT DOES MONUMENT DESIGNATION ACHIEVE?

The city's Cultural Heritage Ordinance has gone through several amendments since 1962. For example, the Cultural Heritage Board was converted into a full-fledged Cultural Heritage Commission (CHC) during the 1980s, which then gave the Los Angeles City Council the final vote on designating a Historic-Cultural Monument (HCM). But the basic contours of the city's historic designation program have remained constant since 1962.

In part, HCM designation confers honor and recognition on historic sites, fostering a sense of place and time and enhancing civic pride. Designation also provides some protection to the designated building or place. It triggers a requirement that the CHC review any proposed substantial alterations to the building or site, in accordance with nationally accepted historic preservation standards. Designation also allows the CHC to delay a proposed demolition: the Commission may object to the issuance of any demolition permit for 180 days, with an additional 180-day objection period (for a total of 360 days) possible upon approval of the city council.

Contrary to the widespread public belief that designated historic landmarks cannot be demolished or altered, HCM designation does not provide iron-clad protection: even demolition is still possible, after the delay period ends. Almost all local preservation ordinances allow for demolition of designated landmarks if it can be demonstrated that designation would preclude the economically viable use of a property, since a

THE LEONIS ADOBE, 23537 CALABASAS RD., ON THE WOODLAND HILLS/CALABASAS BORDER, HCM #1

LYTTON SAVINGS, 8150 SUNSET BLVD., SUNSET STRIP, HCM #1137, 1960

"taking" of property is prohibited by the Fifth Amendment of the U.S. Constitution, which states, ". . . [Nor] shall private property be taken for public use, without just compensation." But Los Angeles's ordinance is also somewhat weaker than those in other cities by only allowing its preservation commission to delay, and not fully deny, a demolition proposal.

As a result, a handful of HCMs have been demolished over the years. For example, Lytton Savings, a Mid-Century Modern style bank building from 1960 located at 8150 Sunset Blvd and designed by Kurt Meyer, was designated as HCM #1137 in 2016. However, soon after its designation, the city council also approved a replacement project for this site, a mixed-use development designed by architect Frank Gehry. The CHC exercised its authority to delay the demolition, to explore the feasibility of relocating the bank building to another site. However, when these efforts proved unsuccessful, demolition of the bank was set to proceed in 2021.

But even though the city council and CHC may only object to a demolition for just under a year, demolitions of HCMs are nevertheless rare. Under the California Environmental Quality Act (CEQA), the proposed demolition of a historic site usually requires the preparation of a full environmental impact report, a detailed analysis that includes an evaluation of the feasibility of preservation alternatives. The considerable time (typically about one year) and expense of preparing an environmental impact report provides an additional deterrent to pursuing demolition.

WHAT CAN BE DESIGNATED AS A HISTORIC-CULTURAL MONUMENT?

Contrary to common belief, the age of a building or site does not, in itself, deem it significant or eligible for designation. Not all older buildings are worthy of HCM status, and not every designated HCM is "old."

Unlike the National Register of Historic Places, which requires that properties less than fifty years old

■ CINERAMA DOME, 6360 SUNSET BOULEVARD, HOLLYWOOD, HCM #659
■ THE DEODAR CEDAR TREES ON WHITE OAK AVENUE IN GRANADA HILLS, HCM #41,
WERE AMONG THE FIRST GROUPINGS OF TREES TO ACHIEVE HCM STATUS, IN 1966.

must demonstrate "exceptional importance" to be listed, the City of Los Angeles has no minimum-age requirement for designation.

Los Angeles therefore has a tradition of openness to "young" landmarks. The Cinerama Dome in Hollywood opened in 1963 and was designated HCM #659 in 1998, only thirty-five years later. The Greek Orthodox Saint Sophia Cathedral opened in 1952 and was designated HCM #120 in 1973, just twenty-one years after its opening. *Binoculars*, the art work by Claes Oldenburg and Coosje van Bruggen framing the entrance to the parking garage at the Chiat/Day Building in Venice, was only nine years old (and became the first landmark from the 1980s) when it was designated HCM #656 in 1998.

Typically, the only time consideration for HCM designation is whether enough time has passed to provide sufficient perspective on a proposed HCM's significance.

HCM designation is not limited to buildings; the list of Historic-Cultural Monuments includes bridges, stairways, traffic medians, and public art, as well as open spaces such as MacArthur Park and Echo Park. Other examples of HCMs include Eagle Rock (the giant rock that gave its name to its eponymous community), the Stoney Point rock outcroppings of Chatsworth, a grouping of deodar cedar trees in Granada Hills, and the Aoyama Tree (a Moreton Bay Fig tree in Little Tokyo).

NOMINATING AN HCM

HCM nominations may be initiated through an application, submitted by anyone—a property owner, preservation organization, historical society, or any organization or individual. Nominations may also be initiated by the city council (typically through a council motion introduced by the member representing the district of the proposed site), the Director of Planning, or the CHC itself.

In the City of Los Angeles, unlike some cities,

PRESERVATION PROFILE:
GAIL KENNARD

Gail Kennard was appointed to L.A.'s Cultural Heritage Commission in 2010 and became the Commission's vice president in 2014. After beginning her career as a journalist for United Press International and Time Magazine, *she joined her father's firm, Kennard Design Group (KDG), the oldest African American-owned architectural practice in the western United States, as director of communications in 1987 and then as president beginning in 1995.*

I'm a second-generation native Angeleno and grew up as the daughter of an architect. My father was a Modernist—he was a student of Richard Neutra—and when I was appointed to the Cultural Heritage Commission, I felt an obligation to save the Modernist architecture that he loved so much. Much of that architecture doesn't have the elaborate, ostentatious look that preceded it, and it was about providing housing for middle-income, everyday folks. Plus, I was very concerned that these types of buildings, and the histories behind why they existed in the first place, would be lost.

The narratives of people of color or indigenous peoples have not always been part of the history that's told. The folks who have the mouthpieces—the wealthier people—get to tell the story. I was at a conference and heard a story about a father who used to read bedtime stories to his little son about a lion and a man. The little boy asks, "How come the lion never wins?" And the father says, "The lion will win when he gets to tell his own stories." We've had a constant stream of people from all over the world who've made Los Angeles what it is today, and it's very important to tell those stories—to save and document that history.

One of the stories that I thought was important was Parker Center, the headquarters of the Los Angeles Police Department, designed in the 1950s by Welton Becket. On one hand, it represented the modern age of policing and new technology; and on the other hand, you had the huge racial disparities in the police department and the LAPD acting in ways that were detrimental to communities of color. The city itself wanted to demolish the building to make way for new city offices. Our commission initiated the nomination for Parker Center: we stepped in ourselves and tried to save it—unsuccessfully. There wasn't support for Parker Center from any of the communities of color—everyone wanted it razed because it had that painful history. How do we deal with structures that have a fraught history? I just didn't feel the building itself should have been the victim. But I think the lesson of Parker Center was that it's important to document those histories and preserve and reuse these buildings even though they have difficult histories. If we don't document them, then we're doomed to repeat the mistakes of the past.

I think it's really important that we're designating properties that show the history of our city. If we don't save the buildings that reflect that history, the city is diminished. The buildings can show that in a way a history book can't—they're a physical representation of something significant that happened here, socially and culturally. ✖

ECHO PARK, HCM #836

designation as an HCM does not require consent of the property owner. Property owners who are opposed to designation may participate actively in all public hearings at the CHC and city council, and some choose to retain attorneys or consultants to help make the case as to why they believe their property does not warrant HCM status. Nevertheless, a vast majority of HCM nominations are supported by property owners, and, more often than not, are actually submitted by property owners themselves. Many owners see HCM designation as a way of highlighting the architectural qualities and historic significance that they cherish about their properties, and as a way to help preserve their property for future generations.

Other property owners are additionally motivated

STONEY POINT OUTCROPPINGS, CHATSWORTH, HCM #132

FRANKLIN AVENUE BRIDGE (SHAKESPEARE BRIDGE), FRANKLIN HILLS/LOS FELIZ, HCM #126

by a financial incentive: designation of a property as an HCM makes it eligible to participate in the Mills Act Historical Property Contract program, a state law administered by local governments. Voluntary participation in the Mills Act program can result in a significant property tax reduction in exchange for a ten-year commitment to reinvest the savings in substantial rehabilitation work.

WHAT ARE THE CRITERIA FOR HCM DESIGNATION?

The city's three criteria for designation are fairly straightforward. A proposed HCM does not need to meet all three criteria to be eligible; it only needs to meet one.

Office of Historic Resources staff prepare a professional staff recommendation for consideration by the CHC, evaluating the nomination by each of the following criteria:

Association with Historic Events or Social/Cultural History

The first criterion addresses historic events and broad historic patterns, evaluating whether the proposed HCM is "identified with important events of national, state, or local history or exemplifies significant contributions to the broad cultural, economic, or social history of the nation, state, city, or community."

Sometimes these historic associations are tied to a specific event. The site of Campo de Cahuenga, HCM #29, was recognized as the location of the treaty signing that ended the Mexican-American War in California and led to California's transfer from Mexican to American rule. Other times, the association may be with a series of events: Venice West Café, HCM #979, was designated as a significant gathering place for the Beat Generation, which influenced the development of mid-twentieth century Bohemian counterculture in the Venice community in the late 1950s and early 1960s.

This criterion's language also allows for the designation of places that reflect the broader cultural history of Los Angeles. The Bob Baker Marionette Theater, HCM #958, was designated in great part for its more than half-century of association with puppeteering in Los Angeles, entertaining generations of Los Angeles families.

■ CAMPO DE CAHUENGA, UNIVERSAL CITY, HCM #29
▪ VENICE WEST CAFE, 321 S. OCEAN FRONT WALK, HCM #979

Association with "Historic Personages"

The second criterion for HCM designation evaluates whether the property is associated "with the lives of historic personages important to national, state, city, or local history."

Some "historic personages" are political figures, such as Ralph J. Bunche, the Nobel Prize-winning diplomat whose boyhood home in Southeast Los Angeles is HCM #159, or two-time Democratic presidential nominee Adlai E. Stevenson II, whose birthplace, a West Adams house, is HCM #35.

The criterion for "historic personages" demands that the CHC and city council determine the historic importance of an individual, the strength of an individual's association with a property, and the ability of the associated place to convey its significance. Determining who qualifies as a "historic personage" does involve some judgment, and sometimes engenders lively debates. In 2017 and 2018, the HCM nomination of the Aidlin-Rees Apartments in the Beverly-Fairfax District significantly hinged upon whether Rudolf Ising, who resided at the property from 1936 to 1939, qualified as a historic personage because he was the co-creator of *Looney Tunes* cartoons. Although OHR staff recommended against designation on this basis, the Cultural Heritage Commission approved its designation on a split vote, finding that Ising's animation achievements qualified him as a historic personage. However, the city council ultimately rejected the nomination, swayed in part by arguments from the property owner's attorney that Ising's early cartoons perpetuated racial stereotypes.

The Charlotte and Robert Disney House in Los Feliz, HCM #1132, was designated for its association with Walt Disney; although Walt lived there with his brother, Robert, for less than a year, it was where he created his first animation studio, which would grow into the Disney empire. In contrast, a Valley Village apartment where a teen-aged Norma Jean Dougherty lived for one year with her in-laws during World War II, before she became famous as Marilyn Monroe, was declined for HCM designation since the apartment's association with her productive career was not strong, and because she lived in many other Los Angeles-area residences during her years of public prominence.

THE STAHL HOUSE
(CASE STUDY HOUSE
#22), 1635 WOODS DR.,
HOLLYWOOD HILLS,
HCM #670 (1960)

■ PERFORMANCE CIRCA 1960 AT THE BOB BAKER MARIONETTE THEATER, 1345 W. 1ST ST., WESTLAKE, HCM #958
▨ CHARLOTTE AND ROBERT DISNEY HOUSE, 4406 KINGSWELL AVE., LOS FELIZ, HCM #1132

Architectural Style

The highest percentage of buildings listed as HCMs were designated because they embody "the distinctive characteristics of an architectural style." The Stahl House (Case Study House #22), HCM #670, best known for the Julius Shulman photograph of the home floating above the L.A. basin, was designated as an iconic example of a Mid-Century Modern residence. La Casa de las Campanas, HCM #238, in Hancock Park, is an outstanding example of Spanish Colonial Revival residential architecture.

Other HCMs are designated because they embody a property type, rather than a specific architectural style. Wurfl Court in Echo Park (HCM #1142) was found to be an excellent example of a housing type that is distinctively Southern Californian: the multi-family bungalow court. The Munch Box (HCM #750), a small 1950s hamburger stand in Chatsworth, was designated as an excellent example of a walk-up food stand.

LA CASA DE LAS CAMPANAS, 350-354 N. JUNE ST., HANCOCK PARK, HCM #239

The second part of the design criterion evaluates whether the proposed HCM "represents a notable work of a master designer, builder, or architect whose individual genius influenced his or her age." Numerous HCMs have been designated based on associations with master architects, including Laurelwood Apartments (HCM #228) by R.M. Schindler in Studio City, the Ennis House (HCM #149) by Frank Lloyd Wright in the Hollywood Hills, and Richard and Dion Neutra's VDL Research House (HCM #640) in Silver Lake.

■ THE MUNCH BOX, 21532 DEVONSHIRE ST., CHATSWORTH, HCM #750
■ THE ENNIS HOUSE, 2607 GLENDOWER AVE., LOS FELIZ, HCM #149

PRESERVATION PROFILE: BOBBY GREEN

Bobby Green, together with his partners, Dimitri Komarov and Dmitry Liberman, formed the 1933 Group in 1999. Since then, the team has created several unique bars in the Los Angeles area, each with a strong design aesthetic. The 1933 Group's projects have put reuse of historic buildings at the heart of their company's business strategy.

When I was ten years old, I moved here with my family from Oklahoma. Coming from Oklahoma to the heart of L.A. back in 1980 was like a trip to Disneyland: there was still tons of interesting flavor and quirkiness all around town. You still had lots of Googie, there was the Hamburger That Ate L.A. (on Melrose), the Frank Gehry building with the binoculars—so there was a lot of new programmatic architecture popping up, mixed with the old. L.A. was like this giant movie set, a fantasyland.

Going to junior high school in Studio City, I remember seeing the Idle Hour—it was then called La Caña. It was never open, and just slowly became dilapidated. We purchased it at auction. The L.A. Conservancy Modern Committee was instrumental in us getting the property. They showed up the day of the public auction with a piece of paper to hand out to everyone

there explaining that the building was landmarked, that it couldn't be torn down. Once the bidding started, whenever we raised our hand to raise the bid, everyone from the Conservancy would clap.

We spent $2 million on the barrel, but it's worth it. There's instant history and a strong foundation that someone opening a new bar or restaurant would have to build on their own. It does come with pressure and concern from many people and groups, so you have to be careful and do it right. It's worth the extra time. There's just a lot more meat on the bone, a lot more to talk about, and more for the press to grab onto.

We got the [Bulldog Café] from the Petersen Museum. I just started brainstorming and found it could be cut into pieces and trucked over to our project and put back together. I couldn't *not* do it—it's too cool. It's just another layer to teach people about the programmatic architecture that was once everywhere in L.A.

The place I've done that hits people the most is the [Highland Park Bowl]—just the grandeur of it, that it's unlike any bowling alley you've been to in your life. The lanes are original, the walls, ceiling, and floor are original. A lot of people have no clue what the place was, or its history. But because these places are so unusual, they know they're in something different—it's not cookie-cutter. Everyone's affected by it, whether or not they consciously know why.

I hope that my efforts inspire other people across the country. We're bringing balance to the city. The city has been tilting toward demolition, new buildings, and remodels so heavily that no one's stopped to look around, to tell these migratory people coming through L.A. that it's the story that makes this L.A.—what it looks like, the quirkiness of it all. But I can't do it alone—I get so many calls and emails saying, "This place, that place, you should do this," and I always say, "No, *you* should do it"—we need more people involved in saving these awesome places. ✖

GLEN LUKENS HOME AND STUDIO, WEST ADAMS, HCM #866

Built in 1940 in the West Adams neighborhood, the Glen Lukens Home and Studio was developed as the rear portion of an existing HCM, the Lycurgus Lindsay estate (HCM #496). One of the earliest surviving works of noted Mid-Century Modern architect Raphael Soriano, the house was designed for ceramic artist Glen Lukens, who taught at the University of Southern California's School of Fine Arts. At the time of the house's construction, Frank Gehry was one of Lukens's art students. Lukens brought Gehry to the construction site, where he met Soriano and became increasingly intrigued by architecture.

Lukens lived at the house until 1959, but by 2007, the house was in desperate condition. Drug dealers and vagrants were squatting on the property, utilities had been cut off for twenty years, and the Department of Building and Safety issued an order to demolish the house as a nuisance property. After the order was issued, an inspection of the property with the LAPD left a city attorney sickened with carbon monoxide poisoning following exposure to a portable generator in an unventilated room.

The house was nominated by the West Adams Heritage Association and the Modern Committee of the Los Angeles Conservancy, forestalling the demolition order and ultimately resulting in its designation as HCM #866 in 2007. The property was soon sold to a preservation-minded buyer, Michael Chapman, who retained preservation architect Barry Milofsky of M2A Architects to rehabilitate the home. Chapman and Milofsky were guided by photos that Julius Shulman had taken soon after construction, as well as by Soriano's original drawings, stored in the Cal Poly Pomona archive. The 1908 greenhouse, a remnant of the Lindsay estate, was restored and reused as a dining pavilion. The rehabilitation won a Conservancy Preservation Award in 2013.

A property that had been slated for demolition as a neighborhood nuisance a decade earlier was transformed into a significant landmark and a neighborhood asset. The Lukens House demonstrates how even the most precarious historic properties can make an economic turnaround: Chapman, who had purchased the property in 2010 for $285,000, sold it in 2019 for $1.85 million.

GLEN LUKENS HOME AND STUDIO
AS A NUISANCE ABATEMENT PROPERTY, 2009

■ GLEN LUKENS HOME AND STUDIO, 3425 W. 27TH ST., JEFFERSON PARK, EAST ELEVATION, AFTER REHABILITATION, 2012
■ GLEN LUKENS HOME AND STUDIO INTERIOR AFTER REHABILITATION, 2012
■ LUKENS HOME AND STUDIO INTERIOR AFTER REHABILITATION, 2012

CHASE KNOLLS GARDEN APARTMENTS, SHERMAN OAKS, HCM #683

From the early 1900s through the 1940s, the Chase family in Sherman Oaks operated a dairy that included a bottling and pasteurizing plant. In 1947, as development accelerated after World War II, Joseph Chase decided to develop this family property, hiring Heth Wharton to design a large apartment complex. Notable at the time was that Wharton's design partner was the African American stylist Ralph Vaughn, who later became an architect; they collaborated with landscape architect Margaret Schoch.

The project reflected Federal Housing Administration (FHA) guidelines based on the Garden City movement of planning and urban design, widely credited to Ebenezer Howard in turn-of-the-century England. These guidelines encouraged "super block" developments set back from the street, modern architectural designs, landscaped courtyards, gardens, and the separation of vehicular and pedestrian traffic.

Chase Knolls Garden Apartments executed these principles beautifully, creating 260 units in nineteen buildings, linked by pathways designed around the knoll on which the Chase family home may have once stood. Landscaping was a prominent feature of the site, with over three hundred trees, a variety of shrubs and plants, and manicured lawns. Wharton and Vaughn's design emphasized the creation of communal gathering spaces, fostering a complex that maintained significant social interactions and a palpably tight-knit community.

ENTRYWAY DETAIL AT CHASE KNOLLS

By 2000, Chase Knolls had been purchased by Legacy Partners, which announced plans to demolish and redevelop the property as new condominiums. Legacy offered relocation buyouts to the tenants and began eviction proceedings against the holdouts. After many of the tenants who highly valued the architecture and design of Chase Knolls began to organize, Councilmember Mike Feuer introduced a council motion to designate Chase Knolls as an HCM, with advocacy support from the L.A. Conservancy.

The HCM debate around Chase Knolls became a high-profile preservation battle, with its owner retaining a battery of land-use attorneys, preservation consultants, and lobbyists to defeat the nomination. The outcome of the nomination—and the fate of the Chase Knolls community itself—was still in doubt as the nomination went to the city council floor in July 2000. In the end, the council voted to designate the property as an HCM, blocking the demolition and bringing an end to the tenant evictions. By the following year, Legacy Partners had completed an about-face, entering into a Mills Act Historical Property Contract with the city, providing the owners with a property tax incentive to preserve and rehabilitate the complex.

More recently, under new ownership, six new buildings were added to the Chase Knolls site with 141 additional units, replacing some of the original carports that were considered secondary features.

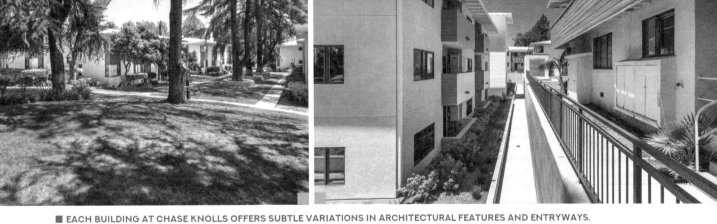

■ EACH BUILDING AT CHASE KNOLLS OFFERS SUBTLE VARIATIONS IN ARCHITECTURAL FEATURES AND ENTRYWAYS.
■ EXTERIOR ENTRANCE TO THE CHASE KNOLLS PROPERTY
■ CHASE KNOLLS GARDEN APARTMENTS, 13401 RIVERSIDE DR., SHERMAN OAKS, WITH ITS AMPLE OPEN SPACE AND LANDSCAPED PATHWAYS
■ NEWER THREE-STORY BUILDINGS AT CHASE KNOLLS HAVE ADDED 141 UNITS TO THE COMPLEX.

■ CENTURY PLAZA LOBBY, 1966
▨ CENTURY PLAZA HOTEL, WITH TWO HIGH-RISE RESIDENTIAL BUILDINGS UNDER CONSTRUCTION, 2020
▧ CENTURY PLAZA HOTEL, 2025 AVENUE OF THE STARS, CENTURY CITY, 2015

CENTURY PLAZA HOTEL, CENTURY CITY, HCM #1060

The twenty-story Century Plaza Hotel, opened in 1966, was the centerpiece of the Century City development created by Alcoa Properties, Inc. as a major new mixed-use center from the former backlot of Twentieth Century Fox Studios. The hotel, designed by architect Minoru Yamasaki, features a unique curvilinear form with a concave eastern façade facing Avenue of the Stars. Yamasaki was one of the most prominent and prolific post-World War II architects in the United States; his best-known work, New York's World Trade Center (1972), was destroyed in the terrorist attacks of September 11, 2001.

Originally designed to accommodate eight hundred rooms, the hotel's Westside location and sleek modern design helped make it a lodging of choice for dignitaries, heads of state, actors, and entertainers. In August 1969, the Century Plaza was the site of a state dinner honoring the Apollo 11 astronauts who had returned from the moon. Broadcast live on national television, the event—with its 1,440 guests—was perhaps the largest and most highly publicized state dinner held outside of Washington, DC. President Ronald Reagan frequently stayed at the hotel whenever he was in Los Angeles; he held his 1980 and 1984 victory parties there.

But by 2009, the Century Plaza was threatened with demolition, to be replaced with a large $2 billion development with two towers of fifty stories each, including condos, retail, offices, and a smaller hotel. The Los Angeles Conservancy launched a high-profile advocacy campaign opposing its demolition, and the National Trust for Historic Preservation named the hotel as one of "America's 11 Most Endangered Historic Places."

Councilmember Paul Koretz's 2009 city council motion to designate the Century Plaza as an HCM served as the catalyst for negotiations among the parties to reach a preservation agreement. The ultimate "win-win" solution, supported by the National Trust and the Conservancy, provided for the rehabilitation and historic designation of the hotel, retaining 400 hotel rooms while converting six of the top floors to sixty-three condominiums. Two new high-rises would be developed to the rear of the hotel and a low-scale retail structure would activate the front of the property along Avenue of the Stars. Once the HCM designation was later approved in 2013, the Office of Historic Resources staff reviewed the preservation and rehabilitation of the building's Mid-Century Modern materials, such as its exterior aluminum panels. The rehabilitated "Fairmont Century Plaza" is slated to reopen in late 2021.

PRESIDENT RICHARD M. NIXON'S STATE DINNER FOR THE APOLLO 11 ASTRONAUTS AT THE CENTURY PLAZA HOTEL, 1969

WEATHERWOLDE CASTLE, TUJUNGA, HCM #841

In 1927, New Orleans native Marcel Dumas designed and built a distinctive home for himself and his wife in the foothill community of Tujunga, along Sunset Boulevard (later renamed Commerce Avenue). They named the house "Chateau de Sales," and it was a French Norman castle complete with leaded glass windows, a floor-to-ceiling fireplace, and a turret with a cantilevered spiral staircase.

Dumas moved from the house by 1930, and several other residents occupied it in the 1930s. After Dumas had apparently stopped paying property taxes on the house during the Great Depression, Jack Harris was able to pick up the house in 1939 by paying off a tax lien (though local lore persisted for decades that the house had been lost in a high-stakes poker game).

Harris's wife, Dixie Ann, was secretary to Hollywood producer David O. Selznick; that and the castle's distinctive appearance and extensive landscaping helped make it a magnet for celebrities during the nearly four decades the Harris family owned the property. Yvonne Kenward, an antique collector and dealer, purchased the property with her husband in the 1970s. She renamed the house "Weatherwolde" (purportedly an Anglo-Saxon term meaning "snug from the weather"), made the property a showcase for her antiques, and heavily promoted the castle's mystique in the local press. The Kenwards sold the property in 1979 to the Hollywood producers/writers Michael Baser and Barbara Stoll, and during their occupancy the castle became hidden by overgrown landscaping.

In the summer of 2005, a developer purchased the property with intention to build new homes on the site. The lot was cleared and the landscaping cut down on a Friday, suddenly leaving an exposed castle on an otherwise vacant lot over a weekend. Several local residents stripped everything of value from the home—from the windows to the spiral staircase—and other community members, led by local resident Gina Zamparelli, swung into action for preservation advocacy. They persuaded Councilmember Wendy Greuel to introduce a city council motion initiating the designation of the castle as an HCM, which was approved over the objections of the developer.

Local musician and preservationist William Malouf became interested in the castle (despite its stripped condition) during the designation process, and after lengthy negotiations on price, was able to purchase it from the developer in the fall of 2005. Malouf steadily began to track down the missing architectural fixtures and features and managed to cajole their "caretakers" to return almost all of them to the house, as part of a thorough multi-year restoration.

The combination of the historic designation and a truly committed new owner have given new life to a notable Tujunga community landmark.

**REAR OF WEATHERWOLDE CASTLE
WHILE THREATENED BY DEMOLITION IN 2005**

ST. VIBIANA'S CATHEDRAL, DOWNTOWN LOS ANGELES, HCM #17

One of the most dramatic preservation rescues in Los Angeles history—the fight to save St. Vibiana's Cathedral in Downtown L.A.—significantly hinged on the cathedral's Historic-Cultural Monument status.

The cathedral is one of the oldest designated landmarks in the city, dating to 1876—a time when its seating capacity of 1,200 could accommodate more than one-tenth of Los Angeles's 10,000 residents. It became the seat of the Archdiocese of Los Angeles and hosted important church gatherings for 120 years, including the 1987 visit of Pope John Paul II. But in 1995, citing damage from the 1994 Northridge earthquake, Cardinal Roger Mahony announced that the archdiocese planned to demolish the cathedral for an all-new cathedral complex on the site.

Early on a Saturday morning in June 1996, the archdiocese began demolition, starting to remove the bell tower's cupola without a demolition permit and without the environmental review typically required to demolish a designated landmark. The Los Angeles Conservancy immediately filed a lawsuit and obtained an emergency court order halting the demolition.

The following month, the archdiocese convinced the city council to approve an action "de-listing" the cathedral as an HCM; city officials then argued that, since the church no longer had designated historic status, no further review of the demolition would be needed. The L.A. Conservancy filed a second lawsuit challenging this action, arguing that the de-listing action itself required environmental review. A superior court ruling ultimately affirmed this argument, and mandated that the archdiocese prepare an environmental impact report before proceeding with demolition.

Cardinal Mahony threatened to build the new cathedral outside of Downtown, or even outside of Los Angeles. But as the legal drama unfolded, a county-owned parcel on Temple Street, a block from Downtown's Music Center, became available; the archdiocese decided to deconsecrate St. Vibiana's Cathedral and build its new complex at that location.

A SATURDAY DEMOLITION ATTEMPT:
REMOVING THE CATHEDRAL'S CUPOLA, JUNE 1996

■ POPE JOHN PAUL II SPEAKING AT ST. VIBIANA'S CATHEDRAL, SEPTEMBER 15, 1987,
JOINED BY THEN-ARCHBISHOP ROGER MAHONY (LEFT) AND CARDINAL TIMOTHY MANNING (RIGHT)
■ ST. VIBIANA'S CATHEDRAL INTERIOR, 214 S. MAIN ST., DOWNTOWN LOS ANGELES, REHABILITATED AS AN EVENT VENUE CALLED VIBIANA
■ VIEW OF THE CATHEDRAL FROM THE CARDINAL'S QUARTERS, THE FORMER RECTORY RESIDENCE OF CARDINAL ROGER MAHONY AND
PREVIOUS LOS ANGELES ARCHBISHOPS, REHABILITATED AS PART OF REDBIRD RESTAURANT

With the historic cathedral now vacant and abandoned, the L.A. Conservancy continued to lead the effort to find an appropriate new use, commissioning a detailed study on reuse options. The National Trust for Historic Preservation included the cathedral on its annual list of "America's 11 Most Endangered Places." This advocacy bore fruit in 1999, when Downtown developer Tom Gilmore agreed to purchase the property, with a vision of transforming the cathedral into a performance and event space. Gilmore and the L.A. Conservancy worked to cobble together funding from several state and federal programs to make the project possible.

Known simply as Vibiana, the building reopened in 2005 and has been hosting weddings, fundraising events, parties, and live entertainment. The former rectory building where Cardinal Mahony once lived and where Pope John Paul II stayed for two nights became Redbird restaurant in 2015, quickly establishing itself as one of Downtown's most prominent fine dining establishments.

IDLE HOUR CAFÉ, NORTH HOLLYWOOD, HCM #977

Decades ago, the Los Angeles commercial landscape was dotted with fanciful buildings shaped like hats, dogs, pigs, owls, and hot dogs—a trend that architectural historian David Gebhard dubbed "programmatic architecture," in which the form of the building often reflected its use. While most of these roadside landmarks are now long gone, a 1941 North Hollywood bar shaped like a whisky barrel endures, due in great part to its HCM designation.

The building was commissioned in 1941 by original owner Michael Connolly, a film technician for Universal Studios, and built by engineer George Fordyk as a tap room and café named the Idle Hour Café. Connolly and his wife Irene lived in a second-story apartment built into the head of the barrel section. The couple later divorced and Irene ran the café until the 1960s, after which it was renamed Rudy's Keg. In 1971, the building was purchased by Jose and Dolores Fernandez and reopened as a flamenco dinner theater called La Caña. The restaurant closed in 1984 and, much like the Mother Goose nursery rhyme "There was an Old Woman Who Lived in a Shoe," Dolores grew old living in a barrel, remaining in the apartment until 2009 with a small menagerie while the building deteriorated.

When Dolores moved into a rehabilitation facility in 2010 and the building's future was in doubt, Chris Nichols, a *Los Angeles* magazine editor and long-time preservation activist with the L.A. Conservancy's Modern Committee, successfully nominated the Idle Hour for HCM status. The property was auctioned off in 2011 after Dolores's death and purchased by the 1933 Group, headed by Bobby Green. Green and his partners spent about $2 million rehabilitating the barrel, preserving original stained glass on the ceiling and doors, reclaiming ceiling planks for the bar's floors, and adding an expansive patio around a large ficus tree. The team also relocated to the café's patio a 1960s reproduction of the 1928 Bulldog Café, a small building shaped like a pipe-smoking dog that once sat on Washington Boulevard and subsequently had been on display at the Petersen Automotive Museum.

REPLICA OF THE BULLDOG CAFÉ, RELOCATED TO IDLE HOUR'S REAR PATIO

■ IDLE HOUR, 4824 VINELAND
AVE., NORTH HOLLYWOOD, AFTER
REHABILITATION
■ IDLE HOUR CAFÉ, 1941

DISTINCTIVE LANDMARKS

Like the Idle Hour Café, many of Los Angeles's HCMs are noteworthy in recognizing sites or buildings that are truly distinctive within our sprawling urban landscape—from folk art to noteworthy or quirky architectural designs.

THE GARDEN OF OZ, HOLLYWOODLAND, HCM #996

The Garden of Oz is one of the city's most unique folk art environments, located adjacent to a single-family home in the Hollywoodland neighborhood of the Hollywood Hills.

Gail Cottman, a former journalist, film studio marketing executive, and founder of a television news satellite service, purchased this property adjacent to her home in 1991 with the original intent of expanding her rose garden. She asked her contractor, Manuel Rodriguez, to create a concrete bed for the roses, which he chose to enliven by including inlaid tiles and beads. Inspired by the message in *The Wizard of Oz* that "everyone is their own wizard," Cottman began to evolve the space as a children's folk art/peace garden, initially

creating a "Munchkinland" with a symbolic yellow brick road and a special throne for Dorothy. The garden developed with many tribute "thrones," highlighting musical figures ranging from Duke Ellington to Ella Fitzgerald and Elvis Presley, and dedicated to peacemakers including Rosa Parks and the Dalai Lama.

The artist Beatrice Wood became a close friend of Cottman's and, over a period of twenty years, created several pieces for the garden until her death in 1998 at age 105. More than seventy-five artists have contributed to the garden, including Bill Attaway, Sally Speelman, Irene Zdunczyk, Patty Detzler, Julie Hunter Bagish, and Bill Davis.

Through Gail Cottman's friendship with Kaz Suyeshi and Musako Morioka, survivors of the 1945 atomic bombing of Hiroshima, she and a group of friends from Los Angeles and Japan created "Garden of Us," in Hiroshima, in 1995 on the fiftieth anniversary of the bombing. And each year, on the anniversary morning of August 6, the Garden of Oz hosts a memorial event with "cello and contemplation for world peace."

Cottman occasionally opens the garden to the general public, but otherwise distributes keys to neighborhood residents and artists to experience this very special Los Angeles "secret garden."

GARDEN OF OZ, WITH BEACH GLASS, POTTERY, AND SHELLS AT FOREGROUND PROVIDING A VISUAL CONTRAST TO COLORFUL TILES AND BEADS

SEE OZ
WITH YOUR
HEART
NOT WITH YOUR
CAMERA.
NO PHOTOS
Please!

■ GARDEN OF OZ,
3040 LEDGEWOOD
DR., HOLLYWOOD
HILLS, WITH TREE
AT FOREGROUND
DEDICATED TO
PRINCESS DIANA
■ GARDEN OF OZ,
WITH MUNCHKIN LAND
(AT LOWER LEFT) AND
YELLOW BRICK ROAD
■ DETAIL OF ORNATE
TILE AND BEAD WORK
AT THE GARDEN OF OZ

SEPULVEDA UNITARIAN UNIVERSALIST SOCIETY SANCTUARY ("THE ONION"), NORTH HILLS, HCM #975

The Sepulveda Unitarian Universalist Society Sanctuary in the mid-San Fernando Valley community of North Hills (formerly Sepulveda) is one of the most distinctive Mid-Century Modern buildings in the Valley. Built in 1964 on land that had once been a ranch, the building was designed by architect Frank Ehrenthal—a Unitarian who had studied with architect Richard Neutra—in a circular shape resembling an onion. Immersing himself in the liberal-minded congregation, Ehrenthal intended that his design would allow congregants to face and relate to one another, conveying a sense of equality and community while maintaining a strong relationship between indoors and outdoors.

The site became a center of political activism during the Vietnam War, which the congregation opposed, hosting a speech in 1970 by controversial anti-war activist William Kunstler to a crowd of five thousand. By then known as "The Onion," it had become a safe haven and headquarters for protesters. In 1983, Vietnam veterans used the chapel as their headquarters for local protests against the Department of Veterans Affairs's policy on Agent Orange and the lack of treatment for post-traumatic stress disorder.

The nomination of the sanctuary for HCM status in 2009–2010 involved a partnership between the church leadership, the L.A. Conservancy, and the John F. Kennedy High School Architecture and Digital Arts Magnet, whose students took the lead in researching, preparing, and presenting the nomination to the Cultural Heritage Commission.

INTERIOR OF THE ONION, 2015

THE ONION, EXTERIOR OF SEPULVEDA UNITARIAN UNIVERSALIST SOCIETY SANCTUARY, 9550 HASKELL AVE., NORTH HILLS

■ GRIFFITH PARK'S GRIFFITH OBSERVATORY
■ GRIFFITH PARK'S WILSON & HARDING GOLF CLUBHOUSE, CONSTRUCTED IN 1937
■ A PICNIC AREA AT GRIFFITH PARK
■ PRESERVED STONE ANIMAL ENCLOSURES AT GRIFFITH PARK'S OLD ZOO, WHICH OPERATED FROM 1912 TO 1966

PRESERVING CIVIC LANDMARKS

Even beyond obvious city-owned historic structures such as Los Angeles City Hall or the Watts Towers, HCM status is helping to recognize and protect a wide range of civic landmarks that are integral to defining the identity of Los Angeles.

GRIFFITH PARK, LOS FELIZ, HCM #942

HCMs may encompass not only buildings, but also large-scale landscapes. Los Angeles's largest park, Griffith Park—stretching over 4,000 acres and featuring dozens of significant historic features—became the largest designated municipal historic landmark in the nation with its HCM designation in 2009.

The nomination was submitted in 2008 by Griffith Van Griffith, great-grandson of the park's original donor, Colonel Griffith J. Griffith, and had the support of park advocates, concerned by proposals that had been emerging in planning for the park's future. While some of the park's historic components, including the Fern Dell Nature Area's Gabrieleño Indian site (HCM #112), the 1853 Feliz Adobe (HCM #401), the iconic Hollywood Sign (HCM #111), and Griffith Observatory (HCM #168), already had separate historic designations, the 2008 nomination took in the entirety of the park.

The historic features highlighted in the nomination and now receiving fuller protection include:

- Municipal Plunge, the largest public pool in the City of Los Angeles, along with its two-story Spanish Colonial Revival style pool house.
- L.A. Live Steamers and Walt's Barn (1950), an open-air collection of rideable 1/8 scale miniature steam, electric, and diesel trains around steel tracks, which includes a line donated by Walt Disney.
- Travel Town Transportation Museum (Collection, 1952–1962), which features an assortment of steam locomotives, cabs, and railway cars.

- Wilson & Harding Golf Courses (1923–1924), meant to serve the public at a nominal cost, with a two-story Golf Clubhouse (1937) that was a product of the 1930s WPA.
- Old Zoo Buildings (1914–1937), featuring a series of cave-like spaces recessed into the side of a hill, with an irregular arrangement of boulders that gives them a prehistoric appearance.
- Merry-Go-Round (1926, installed 1937), which was relocated from San Diego's Mission Beach Park in 1937, Walt Disney's visits to the Merry-Go-Round with his children significantly influenced the creation of Disneyland.
- Greek Theatre (1930), one of Los Angeles's most notable historic outdoor performance spaces and concert venues.

During Griffith Park's designation process, the city's Recreation and Parks Department and Department of Water and Power (which has key facilities within the park's boundaries) sought and received assurances that designation would not prevent needed repairs and upgrades. In the decade since the park achieved HCM status, the designation has not impeded its daily operations or continued evolution.

LOS ANGELES RIVER BRIDGES

Los Angeles boasts one of the nation's finest ensembles of historic bridges, spanning the Los Angeles River, which defined the heart of the city before its channelization following major flooding in 1938. The river bridges, built between 1909 and 1944, were mostly constructed by the City of Los Angeles Bureau of Engineering under the leadership of Merrill Butler, who for decades held the title "Engineer of Bridges and Structures."

To provide broader recognition and protection of the fuller set of river bridges, the Cultural Heritage Commission in 2007 nominated thirteen L.A. River bridges for HCM status. By early 2008, eleven of the thirteen had received final city council approval. Since three other river bridges (Glendale-Hyperion Viaduct, Fletcher Avenue Bridge, and Macy Street Bridge) had previously been designated as HCMs, Los Angeles now has fourteen river bridges under its local historic designation program.

These historic resources reflect three distinct periods of bridge design. Two early river bridges showcased the principles of the City Beautiful movement, which favored monumental civic architecture through their Beaux Arts design: North Main Street Bridge (1910), the first reinforced concrete three-hinged bridge west of the Mississippi River; and Broadway-Buena Vista Street Bridge (1911), the first open-spandrel bridge in California.

A second phase of bridge construction was financed by a series of city bond measures beginning in 1923, still mostly in the Beaux Arts style: Olympic Boulevard (1925); Seventh Street (1927), a double-decker bridge adding to a lower deck from 1910 that served streetcars; Washington Boulevard (1927); North Spring Street (1928); First Street (1929); and Fourth Street (1931), a Gothic Revival design.

Sixth Street Viaduct (1932) was the first river bridge to embrace the contemporary design trends of Art Deco and Moderne. It was also the largest and longest concrete bridge in Los Angeles, at nearly 2/3 of a mile long.

■ THE ENSEMBLE OF HISTORIC LOS ANGELES RIVER BRIDGES LINKING DOWNTOWN AND BOYLE HEIGHTS (2001): FROM FRONT, THE SEVENTH STREET, SIXTH STREET, FOURTH STREET, AND FIRST STREET BRIDGES
■ THE REPLACEMENT SIXTH STREET VIADUCT UNDER CONSTRUCTION (2020)

RENDERING OF THE REPLACEMENT SIXTH STREET VIADUCT, DESIGNED BY MICHAEL MALTZAN ARCHITECTURE

The final phase of bridge building took place during the Works Progress Administration (WPA) era. Riverside-Figueroa Bridge was a 1939 reconstruction and addition to an original 1927 bridge, in the Beaux Arts style, while the Riverside-Zoo Drive Bridge (1938) was a WPA bridge in the Art Deco-Streamline Moderne style. The HCM designations of the bridges immediately helped influence the city's Bridge Improvement Program, which at the time sought to modernize, widen, or seismically strengthen many older bridges. For the Spring Street Viaduct, the Bureau of Engineering (BOE) initially sought to enhance pedestrian and bicycle accessibility through a widening of nearly forty feet, which would have doubled the footprint of the bridge, removed historic railings, light fixtures, and brackets, and obscured the double-arch span over the river. HCM designation spurred discussions between the BOE and the CHC and OHR staff, resulting in a revised design that created new pedestrian and bike access through a more modest widening on only one side of the bridge, while leaving the other side completely intact.

Designation also enabled a significant public debate over the future of the Sixth Street Viaduct, an important landmark in connecting Los Angeles communities that spanned over 3,500 feet to link Downtown Los Angeles to Boyle Heights. It had become one of the most filmed locations in Los Angeles, visually illustrating a grittier side of L.A., and was the preferred site for riverbed car chases in films and music videos, including the climactic drag racing scene with John Travolta in the 1978 musical *Grease*. However, the original construction of the viaduct had used concrete with a high alkali content, creating an "Alkali Silica Reaction" that had undermined its structural stability by the early 2000s.

The CHC initially requested that the BOE evaluate an option that would involve reconstructing the bridge—an approach taken in Pasadena during the early 1990s with the reconstruction of its Colorado Street Bridge. Ultimately, however, the city council approved the demolition of the Sixth Street Viaduct, which began in 2016, to make way for a new bridge design by the noted architect Michael Maltzan.

THE NORTH BROADWAY BRIDGE, HCM #907

AVALON BOULEVARD MEXICAN FAN PALMS, WILMINGTON, HCM #914

HCMs also help recognize and protect significant natural features and plant life within the city. The Avalon Boulevard Mexican Fan Palms were designated as an HCM in 2007, recognizing 218 palms planted in 1931 as part of a citywide beautification effort for the 1932 Olympics.

The palms reflect the legacy of chewing gum magnate and Chicago Cubs owner William J. Wrigley, who had purchased Catalina Island sight unseen from the sons of Wilmington founder Phineas Banning. Wrigley invested heavily in improving transportation to the island, moving to the foot of Wilmington's Canal Street (soon renamed Avalon Boulevard) the operations of the SS *Avalon* and SS *Catalina* ships. As tourism to Catalina blossomed, celebrities and actors would travel down Avalon Boulevard to their yachts, or to board the SS *Avalon* or SS *Catalina,* so the palms provided a symbolic gateway to Catalina.

While palms often earn criticism today for not providing significant shade benefits, the Mexican Fan Palm (or *Washingtonia robusta*) grows to more than eighty feet tall and helps create a visual identity, or a virtual skyline, for major Los Angeles corridors. In Wilmington, a community that has struggled with economic revitalization and air quality impacts from nearby refineries and the Port of Los Angeles, the Avalon Boulevard palms are a very visible source of local identity and pride.

■ AVALON BOULEVARD'S MEXICAN FAN PALMS (900-1750 BLOCKS OF AVALON BLVD., WILMINGTON) FRAME THE DISTINCTIVE ROOFTOP SIGN OF WILMINGTON'S 1930 DON HOTEL.
■ THE PALMS WERE PLANTED IN 1931 TO WELCOME VISITORS TO THE 1932 OLYMPIC GAMES

CULTURALLY SIGNIFICANT PLACES

HCM designation can also be bestowed upon places with no architectural significance, if they have shaped the cultural or social history of the city or the nation. The city has accelerated its efforts in recent years to ensure that its historic designation program includes places with social or cultural meaning.

BUKOWSKI COURT, HOLLYWOOD, HCM #912

In 2007, when a multi-family complex on DeLongpre Avenue in Hollywood was slated for demolition, the notice caught the attention of Richard Schave and Kim Cooper, who conduct literary tours of Los Angeles. The duo knew that the site was the home of the internationally recognized novelist and poet Charles Bukowski from 1963 to 1972. Built between 1922 and 1926, this courtyard complex appears to have been a ready-to-assemble construction supplied by the Los Angeles-based Pacific Ready-Cut Homes company. Schave and Cooper helped enlist a young preservationist, Lauren Everett, to prepare an HCM nomination for the site.

While Bukowski did have several Los Angeles residences, he resided in this complex from 1963 to 1972 during the most pivotal and prolific period of his literary career. It was at the DeLongpre property that Bukowski transitioned from a postal worker to a writer, completing his first novel, *Post Office*, and also *South of No North*, *Mockingbird Wish Me Luck*, *The Days Run Away Like Wild Horses*, and *Factotum*. The property is also the setting for his novel *Women*, and is frequently directly alluded to in his poetry.

The debate over the proposed designation won considerable press attention, fueled in part by assertions from the property owner's attorney that Bukowski's colorful personal life and political views made the site unworthy of designation. Ultimately, however, the property was designated as an HCM in 2008, forestalling the proposed demolition and attracting a new buyer who

BUKOWSKI COURT APARTMENTS,
5124 DE LONGPRE AVE., HOLLYWOOD

committed to preserving the complex.

Today, the small apartment court is rehabilitated and prominently featured on literary tours of Los Angeles.

THE BLACK CAT, 3909
SUNSET BLVD., SILVER
LAKE, WITH BRONZE
HCM PLAQUE VISIBLE ON
THE BUILDING

THE BLACK CAT, SILVER LAKE, HCM #939

While New York's 1969 Stonewall Riots (also known as the Stonewall Uprising) are frequently cited as the catalyst for the modern gay rights movement, events in Los Angeles more than two years earlier led to significant LGBT activism.

Just after midnight at a New Year's Eve celebration on January 1, 1967, eight undercover LAPD officers raided the Black Cat bar in Silver Lake as LGBT patrons were exchanging celebratory kisses and embraces. During the first minutes of the new year, patrons were beaten and dragged out into the street, and many struggled to resist arrest. Following the melee, fourteen people were arrested for assault and public lewdness.

Weeks later, the Black Cat was the scene of a ground-breaking protest organized by two newly formed organizations, Personal Rights in Defense and Education (PRIDE) and the Southern California Council on Religion and the Homophile (SCCRH). On February 11, 1967, several hundred supporters converged on the Black Cat to participate in what was one of the first U.S. demonstrations to support gay rights.

Two of the men arrested for lewd conduct, Charles Talley and Benny Baker, were convicted and required to register as sex offenders—one for kissing another male and the other for being dressed in women's clothing and briefly kissing other men. With the assistance of the American Civil Liberties Union (ACLU), the two men pursued an appeal to the U.S. Supreme Court, asserting the right of equal protection under the law for homosexual men to kiss in public. Although the Supreme Court ultimately voted not to accept the case for consideration, the suit broke new ground in its legal defense of the civil rights of homosexuals.

Bars under several different names had operated out of the Black Cat space since the 1960s, and by 2008 the building housed a bar with a Latino gay clientele (Le Bar) and was still very intact from its 1960s incarnation. Wes Joe, a Silver Lake resident and LGBT activist/historian, together with preservation consultant Charlie Fisher, researched and spearheaded the HCM nomination of the Black Cat. The building was designated as HCM #939 in 2008. It took several more years for the Stonewall Inn in New York's Greenwich Village to achieve similar historic status: in 2015 it became a New York City Landmark, and in 2016 the Stonewall Inn became the first National Monument in the National Park System associated with LGBT civil rights.

FEBRUARY 11, 1967 PROTEST LED BY PRIDE (PERSONAL RIGHTS IN DEFENSE AND EDUCATION), AFTER THE NEW YEAR'S EVE POLICE RAID OF THE BLACK CAT BAR

SITE OF TUNA CANYON DETENTION STATION, TUJUNGA, HCM #1039

In 2013, the Los Angeles City Council approved HCM designation for a one-acre grove of oak trees—not based on the grandeur of the trees themselves, but because the oak grove was the single remaining, tangible link to a shameful chapter of Los Angeles history: the forcible detention of Japanese Americans during World War II at the Tuna Canyon Detention Station in the foothill community of Tujunga, prior to their relocation to permanent internment camps.

After its beginnings as a Tongva village, the Tuna Canyon Detention Station site had become a Civilian Conservation Corps camp beginning in 1933, which made it easy to convert quickly into a detention station within nine days after the bombing of Pearl Harbor. Tuna Canyon housed Japanese American immigrants, as well as German and Italian immigrants and some Japanese Peruvians.

The camp closed in October 1943, after which the site became an L.A. County probation school for boys. In 1960, a group of doctors purchased the site and built the Verdugo Hills Golf Course, demolishing all of the buildings that had existed during World War II. When the site became threatened in 2013 with a proposed housing development, the Little Landers Historical Society began advocacy for HCM designation, which was formally initiated by Councilmember Richard Alarcon.

Despite the site's overriding historic and cultural significance, the nomination presented a challenge because it no longer contained any structures dating back to the time period related to its significance. This led the Cultural Heritage Commission to decline the nomination, recommending instead that the city pursue interpretation and commemoration of the site's history. However, Councilmember Alarcon recommended (and

■ TUNA CANYON DETENTION STATION, 1943, LOOKING SOUTH FROM THE CAMP'S LOOKOUT POST BARRACKS, 1943
■ BARRACKS AT TUNA CANYON DETENTION STATION, 1943

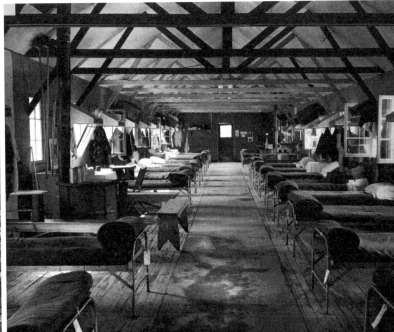

the council adopted) HCM designation for a one-acre oak grove that did remain from the World War II period. The council also requested that the Office of Historic Resources convene a working group to create a community consensus for an interpretive plan for the site.

Implementation of the working group's interpretive plan was delayed several years by a lawsuit filed by the developer, unsuccessfully challenging the HCM designation. During the intervening years, the Tuna Canyon Coalition, bringing together Japanese American leadership citywide and local community leaders, secured a federal grant to create a traveling exhibition on Tuna Canyon's history.

The city council rejected the proposed housing development in December 2019, after local Councilmember Monica Rodriguez asserted that the new project, adjacent to hillsides, would be a wildfire risk. The developer filed a new lawsuit challenging this action, leaving the future of the site in limbo.

NEW TEMPLE MISSIONARY BAPTIST CHURCH, SOUTH LOS ANGELES, HCM #1194

The building at 8734 S. Broadway in South Angeles began in 1932 as a neighborhood movie theater, designed by Clarence E. Noerenberg. A 1944 addition and extensive remodel was designed by the notable African American architect Paul R. Williams. The building was converted to a church in 1956 and became home to the New Temple Missionary Baptist Church in 1966.

But the building became solidified in American cultural history during two nights in January 1972, when singer Aretha Franklin, the "Queen of Soul," chose to record a live gospel concert album, *Amazing Grace*, at the church.

Franklin was joined by gospel performer Reverend James Cleveland, one of Franklin's childhood mentors, and the Southern California Community Choir, as well as her father, Rev. C.L. Franklin. Musicians Clara Ward, Charlie Watts, and Mick Jagger were among those who attended the performance. The album was a tremendous commercial success, becoming the top-selling album of Franklin's fifty-year career as well as the highest-selling gospel album of all time.

Director Sydney Pollack captured the event on film for a concert documentary set to be released in 1972, but the film was shelved due to technical complications. After finally completing the film in 2011, producer Alan Elliott was prevented from releasing it due to litigation initiated by Franklin herself. Following her death in 2018, Franklin's family gave consent to release the film in early 2019.

In conjunction with the film's release and its premiere, Councilmember Marqueece Harris-Dawson introduced a city council motion to designate the church as an HCM. Since California state law had passed in the 1980s ensuring that no religious structure could be newly designated as a local landmark if the religious institution objected, it was important to secure early support from the church. The church's pastor, Rhodell Glasco, immediately embraced the nomination, since that single event had made a lasting impression on the church and the larger community. The church had already converted the room Franklin had used as her impromptu dressing room into a computer lab for youths. The room was dedicated to Franklin and decorated with photos of her albums. The main sanctuary space still looks largely as it did in the film, including the presence of the organ used during the recording.

The Los Angeles film premiere of *Amazing Grace* was held at the church itself on March 31, 2019, with several of the original choir members present. The choir members sang traditional spirituals before the screening, and then sang along with their younger selves appearing on the screen within the same space, providing a vivid and moving testimony to the power of music and the enduring "power of place."

OPPOSITE:
■ NEW TEMPLE MISSIONARY BAPTIST CHURCH, 8734 S. BROADWAY, SOUTHEAST LOS ANGELES
■ NEW TEMPLE MISSIONARY BAPTIST CHURCH SANCTUARY
■ THE ORGAN USED FOR ARETHA FRANKLIN'S *AMAZING GRACE* ALBUM REMAINS IN THE SANCTUARY AT NEW TEMPLE MISSIONARY BAPTIST CHURCH.

CARROLL AVENUE WITHIN
THE ANGELINO HEIGHTS
HISTORIC PRESERVATION
OVERLAY ZONE (HPOZ),
LOS ANGELES'S FIRST LOCAL
HISTORIC DISTRICT

CHAPTER 2
PRESERVING NEIGHBORHOODS:
L.A.'S LOCAL HISTORIC DISTRICTS

If you stand atop the Hollywood Hills overlooking the L.A. basin or the San Fernando Valley, Los Angeles appears to be a vast, daunting city of undifferentiated sprawl. But if you explore the city on the ground—preferably on foot—a very different city comes into focus. It quickly becomes clear that Los Angeles is a city of unique, distinctive neighborhoods, many of which have cohesive architectural character.

A peek down a residential street, often just steps away from a nondescript commercial jumble on a major boulevard, might reveal Craftsman-influenced mansions, collections of bungalow courts, or block after block of intact Spanish Colonial Revival homes. Such an unexpected juxtaposition might make the passer-by exclaim, "I never knew this was here!"

In a city long marked by real estate pressures and rapid change, such neighborhoods do not endure just by accident: their preservation has been the result of concerted grassroots activism and governmental action. Most notably, to help preserve such historic neighborhoods, in 1979 the City of Los Angeles adopted its first ordinance to create Historic Preservation Overlay Zones (HPOZs), which are Los Angeles's designated local historic districts.

Los Angeles now has one of the largest local historic district programs in the nation, with thirty-five HPOZs as of 2020, encompassing over 21,000 properties. Despite the growing reach of the HPOZs, this still only represents just over 2 percent of the approximately 880,000 properties, or legal parcels, across the entire city.

Historic districts are the most effective tool to preserve the unique architectural character of neighborhoods, and also help create a sense of place and community. The concept of historic districts is hardly new—they began in 1931 in Charleston, South Carolina, followed in 1937 by New Orleans's Vieux Carre, created to maintain the historic character of the French Quarter. Today, there are several thousand designated local historic districts across the nation.

In a historic district such as one of Los Angeles's HPOZs, the whole is greater than the sum of the parts. Buildings or properties may not be significant on their

RAINBOW ROW IN CHARLESTON, SC, ON BAY STREET
WITHIN THE OLD AND HISTORIC CHARLESTON DISTRICT,
THE NATION'S FIRST LOCAL HISTORIC DISTRICT

own, or eligible for designation individually; but taken as a whole, the totality has undeniable architectural or historic significance.

The story of L.A.'s HPOZs highlights the tenacious advocacy and persistence of neighborhood leaders who have fought to maintain the history and architectural distinctiveness of their communities. Los Angeles's historic districts represent a productive partnership between these grass-roots leaders and city government, with the Department of City Planning's Office of Historic Resources administering the HPOZ program. Los Angeles's HPOZ program also has several unique qualities that make the city's historic districts quite distinctive when compared with other U.S. cities.

Later in this chapter, a focus on a diverse sampling of five Los Angeles historic districts, large and small, in all geographic areas of the city, provides a glimpse of how historic status has transformed communities and improved quality of life.

THE BENEFITS OF HISTORIC DISTRICTS

Interest in creating new HPOZs has burgeoned throughout Los Angeles in recent decades. In almost two decades following the creation of the City's program (1979–1998), only eight HPOZs were adopted. In the ensuing two decades (1998–2018), the program more than quadrupled, with twenty-seven additional districts adopted. This accelerating interest is a testament to several benefits that neighborhoods receive when they become a historic district.

Protecting Historic Character

Los Angeles's HPOZ Ordinance allows for demolitions of historic structures only when preservation is economically or structurally infeasible, preventing widespread demolitions that can dramatically undermine the historic architecture of other neighborhoods. A historic district also ensures a thorough architectural review of the appropriateness of proposed alterations. HPOZ project reviews apply historic preservation standards that recommend repair over replacement of historic features and materials, or replacement "in-kind" with similar materials where repair is not feasible.

Compatible New Development

Historic district status ensures that proposed new development within the district is reviewed to help make it compatible with the architectural character of the neighborhood. Los Angeles's HPOZs have many good examples of new "infill" development that may include multi-family housing but nevertheless blends well with the historic architecture of its neighborhood.

At the Norwood Learning Village, for example, developer Thomas Safran and Associates and WHA Architects created twenty-nine units of new affordable housing within the University Park HPOZ. The project team broke down the massing into six separate buildings to help blend the new structures into a neighborhood of mostly single-family homes. Each of the six buildings has a distinct architectural identity, taking cues from the building forms, rooflines, and details found in the Victorian-era, Craftsman, and Dutch Colonial Revival architecture within the surrounding neighborhoods.

Tax Benefits

In Los Angeles, owners with "contributing structures" in an HPOZ are eligible to participate in the Mills Act Historical Property Contract Program, the city's most significant financial incentive for owners of historic properties. The Mills Act is a voluntary contract between owners and the City of Los Angeles, which can offer substantial reductions in property taxes that are reinvested into the property to help support substantial rehabilitation work.

NORWOOD LEARNING VILLAGE CREATED COMPATIBLE NEW AFFORDABLE HOUSING WITHIN A HISTORIC DISTRICT BY BREAKING ITS MASSING INTO SEPARATE BUILDING FORMS AND TAKING CUES FROM ARCHITECTURAL STYLES FOUND IN THE UNIVERSITY PARK NEIGHBORHOOD.

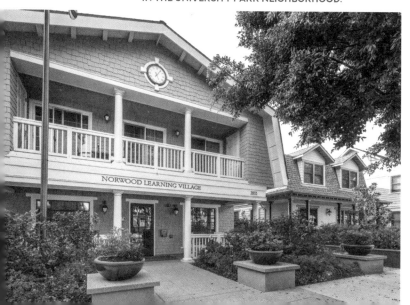

Increased Property Values

The impact of historic district designation on property values is a frequent source of contention in HPOZ adoption debates. But evidence from both Los Angeles and around the nation indicates that historic districts have a modest positive impact on property values, compared with similar neighborhoods not designated as historic. Preservation Positive Los Angeles, a 2020 study on the impacts of historic preservation in L.A. conducted for the Los Angeles Conservancy by PlaceEconomics, further validated this finding for the city's HPOZs.

Some critics of historic districts argue that HPOZ adoption will deter potential homebuyers who fear the additional design reviews or potential delays in obtaining building permits. However, experience has demonstrated that many other homebuyers actually seek out historic districts, in part for their unique character and ambiance, and also because HPOZ designation gives them an assurance that the qualities that initially attracted them to the neighborhood will endure over time.

Enhanced Sense of Community

Working together to form and maintain a historic district often brings communities closer together, giving them a social cohesion that carries over into work on other neighborhood challenges, from neighborhood clean-up to community safety. Many historic neighborhoods already have strong cultural traditions that historic district designation can help to highlight and amplify. And as historic designation also protects the traditional neighborhood design and building forms found in historic neighborhoods, it reinforces a naturally occurring walkable urbanism that fosters more frequent social interaction.

WHAT MAKES LOS ANGELES'S HISTORIC DISTRICTS UNIQUE?

While most major cities have a significant collection of designated local historic districts, Los Angeles's HPOZ program is distinctive and possibly unique in at least four significant ways: its system of volunteer HPOZ boards; its Preservation Plans that guide decision-making in each district; the ethnic and socioeconomic diversity of its historic neighborhoods; and the remarkable variety of architectural styles and settings found among Los Angeles's historic districts.

L.A.'s HPOZ Boards

Given the sheer size of Los Angeles (approximately 470 square miles), it made sense in 1979 to create a system of historic districts that would decentralize their oversight and governance. Each HPOZ was required to have a separate, five-member volunteer board that would hold up to two meetings per month in the local neighborhood. Los Angeles is one of the only cities where historic district projects are reviewed at the neighborhood level, rather than by a single, centralized preservation commission.

Appointments to the board are made by disparate city bodies, to diffuse power and prevent any single city decision-maker from exercising control over the HPOZ. Two of the members are appointed by the city's Cultural Heritage Commission; one of these must be a licensed architect, providing valuable design expertise to the board's deliberations. The mayor appoints a member with real estate or construction expertise—typically a realtor or a licensed contractor—offering a background well-suited to inject a "reality check" into board discussions, based on an understanding of construction techniques or real estate market realities. The city councilmember of the district appoints a property owner or resident from the neighborhood, and the fifth member is appointed by the other four members of the board, with input from the Certified Neighborhood Council from the area.

In the last few years, as the number of HPOZs citywide soared to thirty-five, the city council adopted amendments to the city's HPOZ Ordinance, streamlining the program by allowing multiple HPOZs to share a single, seven-member board, with the two additional appointments made by the Cultural Heritage Commission and the local city councilmember.

The board acts as the final decision-maker on certain types of permit applications, typically for smaller projects or proposed minor rehabilitation work. On applications that involve larger additions or more substantial alterations, the board provides advisory input to the Department of City Planning staff, who are the decision-makers.

In addition to its role in making decisions or recommendations, the board provides valuable expertise and guidance to property owners, helping to meet their needs and aspirations while shaping projects to fit better within a historic setting. Since board members typically bring a long history of community involvement, knowledge of other neighborhood projects, and experience with local contractors, they often introduce pertinent information and perspectives to their discussions with project applicants.

Board members play an important role in leading community outreach within HPOZ neighborhoods, helping to inform residents that they live in a historic district and need to consult with the HPOZ Board and staff before doing work on their properties. Board members also serve as the "eyes and ears" of city government on rehabilitation work happening in their neighborhood, notifying city staff of code violations, such as work occurring without HPOZ review.

Since there are over 100 volunteer board members citywide, city staff play an important role in ensuring professionalism and consistency in decision-making. If the local perspective of HPOZ Board members gets taken to an extreme, a board could become overly parochial, or even arbitrary or self-interested. To help counter these possibilities, the Office of Historic Resources works closely with the boards, actively staffing their meetings and providing ongoing training and guidance.

Preservation Plans

Another unique feature of the city's historic districts is that every HPOZ has a unique Preservation Plan, helping guide decisions within the district. The plan serves as a handbook for property owners, as well as for the HPOZ Board and city staff, on what is expected. The document spells out how different types of work are handled—for example, whether a change to a side façade needs to be reviewed by the board or by staff. It also contains a contextual history for each neighborhood, discussing why the neighborhood is significant and providing a summary of its distinctive architectural styles, to give all community members a common preservation vocabulary and point of reference.

At the heart of each Preservation Plan are design guidelines spelling out approaches that are recommended and not recommended for each element of a building or site, including windows, doors, and roofs, as well as additions or new construction on vacant lots. Each plan's guidelines are tailored to its specific neighborhood based on community input, with choices varying based on the distinctive architectural styles or preferences of each community.

For example, while some plans have specific guide-

THE GREGORY AIN MAR VISTA TRACT PRESERVATION PLAN INCLUDES GUIDELINES FOR FRONT YARD LANDSCAPING, TO HELP PRESERVE THE ORIGINAL LANDSCAPE DESIGN BY GARRETT ECKBO, IN ADDITION TO THE MID-CENTURY MODERN ARCHITECTURAL DESIGN OF GREGORY AIN.

lines for front yard landscaping (such as the Gregory Ain Mar Vista Tract, which has important landscape features designed by notable landscape architect Garrett Eckbo), other plans largely exempt landscape from review altogether. Paint color is another area of frequent variation. In the Victorian-era historic district of Angelino Heights, a color palette can be important to defining a district's historic character; but other HPOZs prefer not to review paint color at all, based on the view that paint is easily reversible.

Economic and Ethnic Diversity of HPOZ Neighborhoods

Los Angeles's HPOZs explode the myth that historic districts are limited to elite, upper-income neighborhoods. While some HPOZs, such as Hancock Park and Windsor Square, are in neighborhoods with mostly wealthier residents, the majority of the city's HPOZs have a median income below the citywide median level. In fact, some HPOZ neighborhoods, such as Pico Union and Lincoln Heights, average less than half the citywide median income.

HPOZs are also more likely to exhibit ethnic diversity within the neighborhood. The Preservation Positive Los Angeles study found that HPOZs have a higher share of non-white population than the average non-white share in the rest of the city. Even as parts of Los Angeles are becoming more stratified, historic neighborhoods consistently attract a vibrant mix of residents from all backgrounds and all age groups.

Diversity of Settings

In addition to the remarkable diversity within each HPOZ, Los Angeles's HPOZs are distinctive for the unusual diversity of settings and characteristics among

THE PHILLIPS HOUSE AT 1300 CARROLL AVE., AN 1887 EASTLAKE/ QUEEN ANNE DESIGN BY JOSEPH CATHER NEWSOM WITHIN THE ANGELINO HEIGHTS HPOZ, IS ALSO HCM #51.

the various local historic districts. While the majority of HPOZs are located within several miles of Downtown Los Angeles (from where the city historically began to expand outward), today L.A.'s HPOZs cover all corners of the city.

In fact, one HPOZ is located at the city's northernmost point in the North San Fernando Valley (the Balboa Highlands HPOZ in Granada Hills), and two others can be found at the southern tip of Los Angeles, in the Harbor communities of San Pedro (the Vinegar Hill HPOZ) and Wilmington (the Banning Park HPOZ). Though most historic districts are within denser communities, such as Hollywood or the Mid-Wilshire neighborhoods, others are in less traditional "historic" settings—including three within the San Fernando Valley, well-known for its suburban development patterns.

The rustic, semi-rural Stonehurst HPOZ in the Northeast San Fernando Valley community of Sun Valley even features large horse-keeping lots, with small stone-clad bungalows constructed by a local artisan and stonemason using rocks from the local washes and foothills.

CREATING A NEW HISTORIC DISTRICT

The adoption of a new historic district is a bottom-up process, spurred by grassroots organizing among community members that offers a way for local residents to chart a course for their neighborhood, shaped by architecture and history. Frequently, the impetus to request a historic district is some type of galvanizing event—perhaps the demolition of a long-beloved structure, or a series of threats, such as an overall neighborhood trend toward "McMansions" or inappropriate alterations.

While the energy behind a historic district is generated from the bottom up, it is also a top-down political process. In Los Angeles, success typically relies upon political support from the city council and, particularly, the city councilmember who represents the neighborhood. Most HPOZs are formally initiated by a city councilmember introducing a council motion, directing that the neighborhood be studied for potential HPOZ status.

To lay the groundwork for an HPOZ, a historic resources survey must be prepared for the neighborhood, evaluating whether the proposed district retains a sufficient concentration of intact historic architecture to qualify for historic

A LAWN SIGN OPPOSING APPROVAL OF THE MIRACLE MILE HPOZ, 2016 (THE HPOZ WAS ULTIMATELY APPROVED BY THE CITY COUNCIL IN 2017).

designation. Once the survey is completed, adoption of an HPOZ involves considerable community outreach and education, typically conducted initially by a local neighborhood organization, and later by the city's Office of Historic Resources. Community meetings help demystify the process and address potential concerns or misconceptions. For example, it is important for property owners to understand that they may make changes to a property's interior, such as a kitchen or bathroom remodel, without HPOZ review; the HPOZ will only review permits for projects affecting the exterior of properties or involving new construction outside the existing building envelope.

Nevertheless, a proposed HPOZ rarely has unanimous support in the neighborhood, as some property owners typically express concerns that the HPOZ will unduly restrict what they would like to do with their property. In some neighborhoods, the property rights objections become amplified, with opponents to the HPOZ organizing themselves in opposition. The most contentious HPOZ debates can resemble a political campaign, with door-to-door canvassing for support or opposition, or even lawn signs advocating pro or con. While some proposed HPOZs do not move forward if there is significant opposition (the proposed Holmby-Westwood HPOZ near UCLA did not proceed to adoption in 2016), those with broad community support move on to approvals at the city's Cultural Heritage Commission, City Planning Commission, and City Council.

SPOTLIGHT ON LOS ANGELES'S HISTORIC DISTRICTS

Each of the thirty-five Los Angeles HPOZs that has successfully navigated the adoption process provides an important slice of the L.A. story, offering a simultaneous sense of history, transformation, and possibility anchored in architecture and culture. Shining a spotlight on five of the city's local historic districts—Angelino Heights, Jefferson Park, Highland Park, Lincoln Heights, and Balboa Highlands—offers a glimpse into the distinctive past, present, and future of L.A.'s historic neighborhoods.

ANGELINO HEIGHTS: L.A.'S PIONEERING HISTORIC DISTRICT

Los Angeles's first HPOZ was established in 1983 in Angelino Heights, which showcases the city's largest collection of Victorian-era architecture. Its HPOZ status came approximately a hundred years after the community was founded as one of Los Angeles's earliest suburbs—a product of the "Boom of the '80s" (which refers to the 1880s, rather than the 1980s).

L.A.'s explosive population growth during this period was fueled in part by the completion of the Southern Pacific Railroad's link to Southern California in 1875. Migration to L.A. accelerated, and the city's population grew from 11,183 in 1880 to 102,479 by 1900, according to U.S. Census Bureau data. And one of the areas where the newly arriving professional class made their home was Angelino Heights.

Angelino Heights lies about two miles northwest of the heart of Downtown Los Angeles, near the community of Echo Park. The neighborhood offers a variety of Victorian-era architectural styles typical of 1880s and 1890s residential neighborhoods, peppered with Craftsman and Mission Revival styles that were added during a second wave of development just after the turn of the

■ THE ITALIANATE FOY HOUSE (1872) AT LEFT WAS MOVED TO 1337 CARROLL AVE. IN 1920, WHILE THE INNES HOUSE (1887), AT RIGHT, FEATURES CLASSIC VICTORIAN-ERA DETAILS AND WAS FEATURED IN THE POPULAR TELEVISION SHOW *CHARMED*.
■ ANGELINO HEIGHTS FEATURES MORE THAN VICTORIAN-ERA ARCHITECTURE: THE 1400 BLOCK OF CALUMET AVENUE IS ONE OF SEVERAL STREETS IN THE HPOZ WITH TURN-OF-THE-CENTURY BUNGALOWS AND PERIOD REVIVAL STYLES.

century. The 1300 block of Carroll Avenue has the highest concentration of Victorian homes in the city and earned a listing on the National Register of Historic Places, while surrounding streets such as Kensington Road and Kellam Avenue contain many other fine examples.

The founders of the Angelino Heights HPOZ broke new ground for homeowners and policymakers alike. The HPOZ co-founder Danny Munoz, who passed away in 2017, spoke about these efforts in an interview with the Office of Historic Resources for the district's thirtieth anniversary in 2013:

> The community approached then-Councilman John Ferraro for support in creating a historic district. The Council Office was supportive at the time, but they did not know how to go about creating a historic district. . . . To help gain support for the HPOZ, the core community preservationists educated the neighbors on the benefits of restoring homes and the importance of retaining the character of the neighborhood. Once people saw their neighbors restoring their homes and bringing them back to their original state, the idea of preservation began to catch on.

In 2008, more than two decades after the HPOZ's adoption, it was expanded to extend beyond the main hill of the district to include the lower-lying areas at its base, closer to Sunset Boulevard, Echo Park Avenue, and the Hollywood Freeway, an area of greater economic diversity and more multi-family residents. Encouraging this portion of the neighborhood to embrace the economic and community benefits of historic designation required different outreach strategies, with materials translated into Spanish and an increased emphasis on tools and resources to make rehabilitation economically feasible.

THIS 1893 QUEEN ANNE HOUSE AT 1343 KELLAM AVE. SAT VACANT FOR MANY YEARS BEFORE ITS 2017-18 REHABILITATION.

Years later, this portion of the neighborhood is becoming increasingly more seamlessly integrated into the original HPOZ, ultimately tying the entire community together.

Through its unique sense of place and the economic reinvestment sparked by the HPOZ in a once-neglected historic neighborhood, Angelino Heights led the way for other Los Angeles neighborhoods to capture the benefits of historic preservation.

JEFFERSON PARK: A HISTORIC DISTRICT BUILDS COMMUNITY AND CREATES ECONOMIC VALUE

Building upon an early agricultural legacy with a cohesive architectural character largely defined by the Craftsman bungalow, the Jefferson Park HPOZ, approved in 2011, has sparked significant reinvestment, increased property values, and knit together a diverse community.

For the half-century after California became a state in 1850, Jefferson Park was a largely agricultural community, with farming operations such as a dairy operated by Joseph Starr. Today, Starr's residence is the only remaining remnant from Jefferson Park's early agricultural beginnings (the Joseph L. Starr Farmhouse, HCM #865).

With the arrival of streetcar lines on Adams and Jefferson Boulevards around the turn of the century, the Jefferson Park community suddenly had an easier commute to Downtown Los Angeles. The area was largely subdivided over the following decade, with homes mostly built by individual property owners rather than larger-scale developers. Nevertheless, the neighborhood developed with a remarkable architectural consistency largely in the Craftsman style, in part due to the widespread use of plan books (also known as pattern books) and kit houses.

Jefferson Park has a decades-long tradition of diversity. In 1920, nearly a third of Jefferson Park residents were foreign-born, with many immigrants from Ireland, Germany, and England. African Americans began to move to the neighborhood in significant numbers around 1930, and during the 1930s Japanese Americans also began to settle in the neighborhood, prior to their internment during World War II. Following the war, an increased number of Japanese Americans came to Jefferson Park, and by the 1950s the neighborhood was a mix of Japanese Americans and African Americans. Noted African American trombonist Melba Liston lived in the neighborhood; the Penguins recorded their 1955 hit "Earth Angel" in a Jefferson Park garage studio. During the late twentieth century and early 2000s, an influx of Latino residents came to the neighborhood, creating a population of approximately 50 percent Latino and 35 percent African American residents.

"Friends of the Jefferson Park HPOZ," the neighbor-

THE JOSEPH STARR FARMHOUSE, HCM #865.

■ CRAFTSMAN BUNGALOWS IN THE 3400 BLOCK OF S. 7TH AVE. WITHIN JEFFERSON PARK HPOZ, ALL BUILT BETWEEN 1910 AND 1915
■ THE FRONT YARD LANDSCAPE DESIGN BY RENEE GUNTER ON 30TH STREET IN JEFFERSON PARK DEMONSTRATED
THE POSSIBILITIES OF DROUGHT-TOLERANT LANDSCAPING IN A HISTORIC DISTRICT.

hood coalition that originally spearheaded the HPOZ's adoption and has since remained active, has become a model citywide for how to sustain public outreach that builds HPOZ support and longer-term awareness. During the HPOZ adoption process, every home within the proposed district received a bilingual (English and Spanish) door hanger providing information on the HPOZ. Such outreach efforts helped generate widespread participation and virtually unanimous support for the HPOZ.

Once the district was established, the Friends group created welcome packets for new homeowners outlining the benefits and responsibilities of living in an HPOZ. Even today, the group sends an email to every realtor listing a home for sale in the neighborhood, reminding them that the listing is located in an HPOZ and that this

information must be disclosed to potential buyers. The group has also created customized signs and placed them at every gateway street entering the neighborhood, identifying it as a historic district and creating a visual cue that this is a special area.

The Jefferson Park story also demonstrates the positive economic impacts of HPOZ designation. When the HPOZ was created during the economic downturn in 2011, most modest single-family Craftsman homes were selling for between $200,000 and $300,000. By 2019, the same homes were largely selling between $700,000 and $900,000. While this increase owed much to the overall strength of the real estate market, the bounce-back in home prices within the HPOZ exceeded the rate of appreciation in other nearby neighborhoods that lacked historic status.

HIGHLAND PARK/GARVANZA: A SPRAWLING HISTORIC DISTRICT WITH AN ARTISTIC SENSIBILITY

Highland Park/Garvanza is Los Angeles's largest HPOZ, with 4,000 properties winding through the Arroyo Seco in Northeast Los Angeles. While the Highland Park neighborhood has been in transition, with new restaurants, retail, and nightlife, the HPOZ has anchored this change in a unique architectural, artistic, and cultural sensibility that defined a distinctive "Arroyo culture" from its very beginnings.

Highland Park was one of Los Angeles's earliest suburbs, with development beginning in the 1880s, sparked by the arrival of two rail lines. The community was annexed to the City of Los Angeles in 1895. Soon thereafter, in 1898, Occidental College relocated to Highland Park following a fire that destroyed its original site in Boyle Heights. During this same period, Charles Fletcher Lummis, L.A.'s original renaissance man—author, photographer, city librarian, *Los Angeles Times* editor, founder of the California Landmarks Club, and founder of L.A.'s first museum (the Southwest Museum)—began building his home in Highland Park. The home, El Alisal, a rustic Craftsman house made of Arroyo stone, became a gathering place for writers, artists, and musicians.

In 1897, painter and professor William Lees Judson and his three sons established Judson Studios, another artistic anchor of the community. Judson Studios is the oldest family-run stained glass studio in the nation, offering products hand-crafted by local artisans. It is now run by David Judson, the fifth generation within his family to oversee its operations from their Garvanza studio.

THE HIGHLAND THEATRE (1925), HCM #549, WITH ITS DISTINCTIVE ROOFTOP SIGN RELIT IN 2011, ANCHORS THE LARGEST COMMERCIAL CORRIDOR IN ANY L.A. HPOZ, ALONG N. FIGUEROA STREET, REVITALIZED WITH BARS AND RESTAURANTS.

Highland Park was approved for HPOZ status in 1994 and was the first HPOZ to include commercial buildings, with a walkable neighborhood commercial district along North Figueroa. In 2010, the Garvanza neighborhood to the northeast of Highland Park was added to the HPOZ. The architecture of Highland Park-Garvanza encompasses nearly every style popular from the 1880s through the 1940s: Queen Anne, Shingle, Craftsman, Mission Revival, and Tudor Revival.

Highland Park's convenient location between Downtown Los Angeles and Pasadena, as well as its transit accessibility with two Metro Gold Line stations, have made it a desirable neighborhood for new development in recent years. Highland Park's commercial district has seen a particularly noteworthy transformation, with trendy new restaurants, retail stores, and nightlife sparking community conversations about potential gentrification or cultural displacement. While the retail environment has radically transformed, the demographic makeup of the residential community has changed less dramatically; according to American Community Survey Census Bureau data, Hispanic/Latino residents still represented 74 percent of Highland Park's population in 2018.

But amidst all the changes, the HPOZ has helped maintain the distinctive Arroyo culture that dates to Lummis, supported by a strong neighborhood preservation organization, the Highland Park Heritage Trust. Arts organizations continue to flourish in the community: the Arroyo Arts Collective has provided a lively network for Highland Park area artists for more than three decades. Since 2000, Avenue 50 Studio has offered a creative gallery space grounded in Latino culture, contributing to a vibrant cultural life in the Highland Park community.

■ JUDSON STUDIOS, HCM #62, WAS THE ORIGINAL SITE OF USC'S COLLEGE OF FINE ARTS AND ARCHITECTURE, BUILT IN 1900 AND REDESIGNED IN 1911 BY ARCHITECTS TRAIN & WILLIAMS.

■ HERIVEL HOUSE (LEFT, HCM #370) AND JOHNSON HOUSE (RIGHT, HCM #369) ARE TWO PROMINENT CRAFTSMAN HOMES ON "PROFESSOR'S ROW," THE 4900 BLOCK OF SYCAMORE TERRACE, THAT WAS A FAVORED LOCATION BY OCCIDENTAL COLLEGE FACULTY BEFORE THE SCHOOL MOVED TO EAGLE ROCK IN 1914.

PRESERVATION PROFILE: RENEE GUNTER

Renee Gunter is a resident in the Jefferson Park HPOZ and an award-winning landscape designer of drought-tolerant gardens, including many for historic homes. In 2013, she also launched a mobile organic produce service, delivering fresh fruits and vegetables to residents of South Los Angeles.

I had been living in the Valley for at least twenty years and decided in 2004 that I wanted to be in an environment that was more culturally rich. I wanted my daughter to experience a community like the one I grew up in. When I moved in, I gave myself a year to look around and figure out what I could contribute to this community. So I started by walking around and meeting people to figure out how I could create a drought-tolerant garden for myself.

My house was the lab for my particular inclination and philosophy for drought-tolerant landscape. The bones are the architecture, so I had to look at how you spotlight the beautiful architecture, the lines, and the history with a garden that blends, supports, and shares the collective street view of the property. It was important to think about the height of plants, the spread, whether they were natives, how they blended with a historic gable, rooflines, or pilasters.

One by one, other neighbors began to realize that it was a beautiful approach and was complementary—it didn't take away from the property and it saved water, which was really important during our drought. Marina Moeves and Steve Peckman's home that I did on Thirtieth Street was the first garden in the DWP rebate program. It won Garden of the Year from the West Adams Heritage Association, and was featured on the front page of the *Los Angeles Times*.

When you start planting, it spreads—it shows what's possible, and it's calming when you walk down the street. You see these beautiful homes with coordinating colors and

gardens that are thriving. You get the sense of a foundation that's worth maintaining and allowing to thrive. That's what creates community.

In 2005, I decided to have a Fourth of July block party. The first year, five or six families showed up, and the next year, twenty. I did this for ten years, and by the end, there were over 800 folks who partied, danced, played games, and got to know each other.

Once these homes are torn down, you don't replace them, you just don't: there goes the neighborhood, as they say. When you saw folks taking an interest and going to the salvage yards to replace features relevant to the year of their house, it really became infectious. You started to see these houses take shape one by one, and then part of a block, and then a whole block. The HPOZ has been an amazing opportunity to restore a part of Los Angeles architecture.

The HPOZ and the landscaping and the community spirit that's been generated as a result of all of that is a benefit to most people, and you can feel it when you drive down the street. People come and go, but a community's core spirit—it's there. We're not the first and we're not the last, but we're a custodian of our homes and our community. I want to pay it forward, to leave my handprint on something that will be remembered, so that people say, "Oh, that was Miss Renee's house." ✖

PRESERVATION PROFILE:
RICHARD BARRON

Richard Barron had his own architectural firm in Los Angeles, Richard Barron/Architects, Inc., for over thirty years. He was a founding board member of the Highland Park Heritage Trust neighborhood preservation organization and of the Highland Park HPOZ, where he served as the board architect for thirteen years. He is one of the longest-serving members in the history of the city's Cultural Heritage Commission, originally appointed in 2005 and serving as Commission President since 2008.

When I was getting my architectural education at Cal Poly Pomona, we dealt with very strict ideas of Modern architecture, and I don't think historic preservation ever came up. After working for several other architectural firms, I went out on my own. The first preservation job I got was in Highland Park—an addition to a little Victorian stone residential building. It was very successful—I picked up on some shingle eave work on the cottage and built the addition with shingles, so that it melded nicely. After that, I worked with the Hollywood Community Housing Corporation on St. Andrews Bungalow Court. It won every preservation award available because it was affordable housing, and it brought back Colonial Revival bungalows that had been in terrible condition. So that became my preservation pedigree.

My office was heavily involved with non-profit housing providers that bought up old buildings. The Boyle Hotel, for example, was really loved by the Boyle Heights community, and it was falling apart at the seams. We ended up putting a concrete building inside the historic building, with shotcrete and rebar from the basement to the roof to hold the brick together. But the building has so much historic significance, and now it provides affordable housing that the community greatly needs, showing how preservation can be a real contributor.

In the 1980s and early 1990s, developers were coming into Highland Park and demolishing nice historic houses on big lots to build very inappropriate and non-contextual apartment buildings. I got involved with the Highland Park Heritage Trust. We'd heard about HPOZs, so we went over and had coffee with Tom Morales, who started the Angelino Heights HPOZ. It took us seven or eight years of tenacious politicking to get the HPOZ. We developed a slide show and took it to a big community meeting: all of the City Council Office deputies came, but we didn't really know how the community would react. And it was an overwhelming success—we had simultaneous translation into Spanish, and many of the longtime Latino residents got up and said they'd lived in the community for twenty years and hated what's going on now.

HPOZs are a healthy planning tool because they democratize land use in the community: they allow the community to participate. I would always say, yes, you're going to give up something to get something: you're not going to have carte blanche to do whatever you want. But at the same time, you're not going to wake up tomorrow morning to find out that your neighbor has completely mutilated his house, and you have to look at it.

I've now been on the Cultural Heritage Commission for fifteen years, and it's been very rewarding. I think preservation is tremendously important. We need to understand where we've come from—our history—and it increases the texture of a city both physically and psychologically. ✳

LINCOLN HEIGHTS: AN L.A. "ORIGINAL SUBURB" WITH A LEGACY OF ACTIVISM

Lincoln Heights is an exceptional neighborhood within Los Angeles based in part on its age: it was subdivided in 1873, making it the city's first residential suburb. Only the nearby Boyle Heights neighborhood still contains a comparable concentration of housing that predates the "boom of the 1880s."

The neighborhood was originally known as East Los Angeles, until the construction of Lincoln High School in 1913. Dr. John S. Griffin and John C. Downey established one of the city's first streetcar lines in 1876 to connect East Los Angeles with Downtown Los Angeles, constructing a road linking North Broadway (Downey Avenue originally) to the Southern Pacific Railroad Depot. The development of the neighborhood proceeded between 1875 and 1929, with the architecture of the homes exhibiting the Victorian, Transitional Arts and Crafts, Craftsman, and period revival styles common during these years.

Initially developed as a neighborhood for the upper middle-class, the neighborhood within its first few decades became attractive to working-class residents and new English, Irish, Yugoslavian, and Italian immigrants seeking employment in nearby industries and in the hospital that opened in 1878 on some of Dr. Griffin's land (which ultimately evolved into Los Angeles County + USC Medical Center).

Along the edges of the Lincoln Heights community were many distilleries, breweries, bakeries, and wineries. In 1903, the Edison Electric Company Steam Plant No. 3, designed by John Parkinson, opened adjacent to the Los Angeles Brewing Company plant along the L.A. River. Pabst purchased the entire brewery in the post-World War II era. The San Antonio Winery (HCM #42), the oldest producing winery in Los Angeles, opened in

■ THE CHURCH OF THE EPIPHANY, DESIGNED BY ARTHUR BENTON, FEATURING GOTHIC-INFLUENCED POINTED-ARCH WINDOWS WITH STAINED GLASS
■ THE BASEMENT OF THE CHURCH OF THE EPIPHANY (HCM #807) WAS A CENTER OF CHICANO ACTIVISM IN THE 1960S AND 1970S.

the neighborhood during 1917.

Lincoln Heights has a rich social history dating back many decades. A large number of Chinese immigrants settled in the neighborhood in the 1930s, together with the construction of a new nearby Chinatown. By the 1960s, Lincoln Heights became a predominately Latino neighborhood, and the neighborhood became a focal point for growing Chicano activism. Lincoln High School played a key role in the 1968 East L.A. "Blowouts" (or walkouts), through which thousands of Mexican-American students protested for civil rights.

A key community center for the Latino community in Lincoln Heights has been the Church of the Epiphany, the oldest sustaining Episcopal congregation in Los Angeles, originally designed in 1887 by Ernest Coxhead. The church constructed a new building in 1913, a mix of Gothic Revival, Mission Revival, and Romanesque Revival styles designed by Arthur Benton, who was also the architect for Riverside's Mission Inn. Beyond its architectural significance, the church has served as a center for social justice. Epiphany was the birthplace of *La Raza*, a newspaper for the Chicano movement that was printed in the church basement, and it served as a meeting place for the Brown Berets, a student activist group. United Farmworkers leaders Cesar Chavez and Dolores Huerta spoke frequently at Epiphany and held organizing meetings at the church. In 2018, after a social media campaign captured over 74,000 online votes, Epiphany was awarded a $150,000 "Partners in Preservation" grant sponsored by American Express and the National Trust for Historic Preservation to assist with the church's rehabilitation. The church was also listed in the National Register of Historic Places in 2020.

The adoption of the Lincoln Heights HPOZ in 2004 was the culmination of many years of advocacy by the Lincoln Heights Neighborhood Preservation Association. With an average neighborhood income of approximately half the citywide median, the HPOZ is using historic preservation as a revitalization strategy, building upon the neighborhood's long tradition of diversity and activism.

BALBOA HIGHLANDS: THE SIXTIES BECOME HISTORIC IN THE SAN FERNANDO VALLEY

The Balboa Highlands HPOZ demonstrates that historic districts need not be particularly "old," or limited to neighborhoods that showcase the architectural styles of the nineteenth or early twentieth centuries. Historic districts can also successfully protect and enhance single-family, Mid-Century Modern homes.

Balboa Highlands is the "youngest" HPOZ in the City of Los Angeles, developed from 1962 to 1964. It is located at the far northern edge of Granada Hills, in the foothills of the Santa Susana Mountains, and is one of only three HPOZs in the San Fernando Valley.

Balboa Highlands was built by the visionary developer Joseph Eichler, who was responsible for thousands of homes in Northern California. It is the only Eichler tract in Los Angeles County and is one of only three groupings of Eichlers in Southern California (along with one tract in Ventura County's Thousand Oaks and three tracts in the City of Orange).

Eichler strived to bring high-end Modernism to the masses, working with notable architects to bring sophisticated architectural designs to communities often marked by uninspiring tract housing. For Balboa Highlands, Eichler worked with architects A. Quincy Jones, Frederick Emmons, and Claude Oakland to design sleek Modernist homes marked by clean lines. The homes varied based on their rooflines, offering a choice of flat, A-framed, or slanted roofs. In almost all the models, the homes were arranged around an atrium accessed through sliding-glass doors, blurring indoor and outdoor space.

Joseph Eichler chose the exterior paint colors for all of his homes; the palette for Balboa Highlands generally featured warm, earth-tone colors for exterior façades with brightly painted front doors, accented by globe

■ 17019 AND 17025 LISETTE ST., TWO SLANT-ROOF EICHLER HOMES, WITH SIGNIFICANT RESTORATION WORK AND DROUGHT-TOLERANT LANDSCAPING ADDED SINCE ADOPTION OF THE HPOZ
■ TWO EICHLER HOMES WITH A-FRAME ROOFS, SET WITHIN A LANDSCAPED SETTING AT THE FOOTHILLS OF THE SANTA SUSANA MOUNTAINS

TWO BEAUTIFULLY RESTORED EXAMPLES OF CONTRASTING EICHLER HOME ROOFLINES: THE A-FRAME ROOF AT 12734 JIMENO ST. (RIGHT), DESIGNED BY JONES AND EMMONS, AND THE FLAT ROOF MODEL AT 12740 JIMENO (LEFT), DESIGNED BY CLAUDE OAKLAND

light fixtures, wood and plaster address numbers, and exposed beams at the roofline.

In an era of restrictive covenants, it was also remarkable that Eichler's Granada Hills tract was open to all homebuyers, regardless of color or religion. According to a *Los Angeles Times* article from 1985, it was the only San Fernando Valley tract outside of Pacoima with a developer-backed policy of nondiscrimination.

The HPOZ came about following the insensitive remodels of several homes during the 1990s. Residents began to highlight the architecture of their neighborhood in a 2000 Los Angeles Conservancy tour of Modern architecture in the San Fernando Valley called "How

Modern Was My Valley," and continued to advocate for an HPOZ over the next several years. To prepare the historic resources survey for the neighborhood, the community worked not only with a professional historic preservation consulting firm, but also with students from the nearby Kennedy High School Architecture and Digital Arts Magnet.

The Balboa Highlands HPOZ serves as a model for other San Fernando Valley and post-World War II communities, showing how a historic district can protect and enhance the unique characteristics of a Mid-Century Modern neighborhood.

PRESERVATION PROFILE: MICHAEL DIAZ

Michael Diaz, a longtime Lincoln Heights resident and property owner, played a leadership role in creating the Lincoln Heights Neighborhood Preservation Association, which spearheaded the adoption of the Lincoln Heights HPOZ. He is a former board member of the Los Angeles Conservancy and the founding president of the Latin-American Cinemateca of Los Angeles, through which he has helped bring classic films from Latin America to Southern California audiences.

In the 1980s, there was a city-sponsored program to give loans for homeowners to rehabilitate their houses. When residents realized the funds were being used to stucco the homes, there was a protest and I became part of a community advisory group that put forward some alternative approaches that emphasized preservation. But the city ultimately scuttled our proposals and went ahead anyway with their own program to give low-interest loans to homeowners to stucco their homes. That's when we formed a group—the Lincoln Heights Neighborhood Preservation Association—to fight the stucco. I had no formal background in architecture; it's just that I lived here and my family owned some properties in the neighborhood.

MICHAEL DIAZ WITH LINCOLN HEIGHTS RESIDENTS STEPHANIE MANCILLAS (RIGHT) AND ALICIA MANCILLAS ROBLES (LEFT)

A number of residents began to see the negative effects of the stucco work, causing us to embark on an educational campaign educating residents about the neighborhood's housing stock and its architectural and historic value. We presented awards to people who maintained their homes properly, without stucco. Residents began to realize they could maintain and upgrade their homes by respecting the original architecture. We designed and distributed a brochure, "Save Lincoln Heights from Stucco," and co-presented an architectural tour of Lincoln Heights with the Los Angeles Conservancy. The city's HPOZ designation gave credence and validation to what the group of activists believed all along.

I'm grateful for the residents who actively participated in educating residents about the neighborhood's historic value and significance: Stephanie Mancillas, Ray Garcia, Jose Luis Sedano, William and Ana Di Cerchio, Seline Seymour, Chip McCarthy, and Vera Padilla, among others. Without them, we never would have had an HPOZ. Credit should also be given to then-Councilmember Ed Reyes, who supported the community activists and, ultimately, the HPOZ.

The HPOZ is now attracting people who appreciate these homes, adding to the fabric of the neighborhood: it's now an interesting combination of Latinx, both the older community and younger Hispanics, plus Asians and Anglos. The HPOZ has contributed to the economic revitalization of the neighborhood in that it is now perceived in a positive light and is a desirable place to live. The HPOZ helped create a positive image of the neighborhood and instill pride in it. ✖

PRESERVATION PROFILE:
ADRIENE BIONDO

Adriene Biondo, a Balboa Highlands resident, was a leader in the creation of the HPOZ, established in 2010. She was a longtime chair of the Modern Committee of the Los Angeles Conservancy (Modcom), focusing her advocacy on preserving and revitalizing examples of commercial architecture in Los Angeles.

We purchased our home in 1995. Even though we looked at over a hundred houses, not one of them gave us the feeling of wonder that the Eichlers did. Our home is the perfect oasis for us—everywhere you look, you can see nature through floor to ceiling "window walls."

At the time I moved into Balboa Highlands, not much was being discussed about the Eichler homes in Southern California, so I contacted a gentleman in the Bay Area named Marty Arbunich who operates a business called the Eichler Network. He offered to add our entire Balboa Highlands neighborhood to his mailing list and sent every homeowner in our community a copy of *CA Modern* magazine, free of charge, for over twenty years. I think that connection has been an important resource in educating homeowners.

In 1999, I overheard real estate agents touring a neighboring Eichler saying, "You can add a second story, or even build a new home here," and that's what tripped the switch for me. At the time, we were planning the "How Modern Was My Valley" tour for the Modern Committee of the L.A. Conservancy, which included the first-ever tour of Balboa Highlands. Over a thousand people toured our home and the five other Eichlers we opened that weekend in 2000. We published our own newsletter called *The Atrium*, started a curb painting program where the address number and Eichler logo was painted at each house, and produced progressive parties and other neighborhood events.

In 2007, as I was heading out to a Sunday dinner with friends, I received a call that a 1958 drive-in restaurant in Downey named Johnie's

Broiler was being demolished. I was well aware of the building, as our group had successfully nominated it as a California State Landmark. Even though we were about fifty miles away in Encino, I told my friends, "I'm sorry, but I have to go to Downey right now." I called everyone I could think of—CBS, ABC, NBC, Downey code enforcement. Analisa Ridenour, who led the Friends of Johnie's group, and I managed to get the sad sight of the demolished Johnie's on CBS News. The City of Downey issued a stop work order along with a moratorium preventing anything from being built on the site for one year. That year gave us enough time to find a new operator, Jim Louder from Bob's Big Boy, who rebuilt Johnie's from the original blueprints—a true phoenix rising from the ashes. The newly rebuilt drive-in has been a tremendous success, appearing on *Mad Men* and other productions.

Preservation is all about connection, mutual respect, and the ties that make a building a treasured part of any community. Buildings have so many stories to share, and that shared history always resonates with me. In my personal role, I think putting a face to historic preservation can make a big difference., A lot of people call me and say, "I didn't know what to do, so I thought I'd call Adriene," and I'm happy to be that face of preservation in my own small way. ✖

CHAPTER 3
FINDING HISTORIC L.A.: SURVEYLA, THE CITYWIDE HISTORIC RESOURCES SURVEY

Historic preservation can only succeed in a city if government officials and community members have a comprehensive sense of what and where their city's historic resources are. For decades, Los Angeles pursued the historic designations described in the previous chapters without taking comprehensive stock of its historic places all across the city.

All of that changed with the 2017 completion of SurveyLA, the Los Angeles Historic Resources Survey. The City of Los Angeles is now able to use survey findings to guide the preparation of long-range plans for each community, and provide a source of important information for developers, property owners, policymakers, scholars, and interested Angelenos.

WHAT IS SURVEYLA?

SurveyLA is the largest, most ambitious citywide historic resources survey in the nation, the result of a lengthy partnership between the City of Los Angeles and the J. Paul Getty Trust. The Getty Conservation Institute (GCI) is renowned all over the world for conserving cultural heritage such as antiquities, Modern architecture, and significant archaeological sites, but its technical support for SurveyLA marked a landmark contribution to its home community. After the GCI undertook an assessment report in 2000 on the need for a citywide survey, the Getty Foundation provided a $2.5 million multi-year matching grant to fund SurveyLA in 2005. The grant agreement between the Getty and the city led to the creation of the city's Office of Historic Resources (OHR) in 2006, since it mandated that the city have a professionally staffed office to oversee the massive survey project. A professional team was hired for the new office, with Janet Hansen bringing deep experience from the City of Riverside and her historic preservation consulting practice to her role as OHR deputy manager. Janet played a key leadership role in the design of SurveyLA tools and methods, as well as the long-term management of all aspects of the project.

CALENDAR LOS ANGELES TIMES SUNDAY, JULY 29, 2007 F7

ARCHITECTURE

ANNIE WELLS Los Angeles Times

THE TIME IS RIGHT: *Ken Bernstein, manager of L.A.'s Office of Historic Preservation, with Deputy Manager Janet Hansen, is leading the cataloging charge, noting historic preservation is "part of a natural maturing of the city."*

Survey has L.A.'s assets in its sights

[*Survey, from Page F1*] that a growing realization that there is importance in historic preservation," says Ken Bernstein, manager of the city's Office of Historic Preservation. "It's part of a natural maturing of the city — or coming of age of the city. And it's become important to catalog what makes Los Angeles Los Angeles."

In 2001 the Getty Conservation Institute published the "Los Angeles Historic Resource Survey Assessment Project: Summary Report," a report that examined preservation in this city. "We were trying to understand if it made sense to even pursue a survey," says Tim Whalen, the Institute's director. "The report indicated that there was a need. What would it require? The problem is Los Angeles is the size of a small country."

Spanning five years and, they hope, the entire city — more than 800,000 legal parcels — the multiphase project launches one of its key elements Aug. 15: an interactive website that will catalog L.A.'s wide-ranging treasures. Some are more evident — historic downtown, clusters of Deco facades, whimsical bungalow courts — others less obvious. Uncovering that "hidden L.A.," identifying what often slips into the margins or can easily be lost to memory, is a key goal of the survey. Ultimately, that information would be available to anyone who might need it, including visiting scholars and deep-pocket developers as well as harried Hollywood location scouts.

"It's a way to bring historic preservation into the 21st century by taking sites that may be considered by some to be nontraditional or that aren't necessarily architectural masterpieces and ensuring that they are reviewed against accepted historic preservation criteria," Bernstein says. Eligibility will be based not only on architectural significance, "but on historic, social or cultural associations." The idea is not to just round up what we think of when we think about Los Angeles — the Neutras, the Schindlers, the Neffs — but to broaden definitions of "valuable."

The project renders the term "significant" more elastic, inclusive. "I think it is an important way to actually change the public's perception about preservation," says Janet Hansen, deputy manager of the Office of Historic Resources. "People generally think that it's about architecture, about things that look good. But this is going to be a really important way for everyone to really understand the goals preservation is trying to reach."

Simply put: "Without a survey, we don't know what we have." This attempt at cataloging, Bernstein says, will help alleviate the panic that can occur when a wrecking ball or bulldozer shows up.

"What we have, I've been calling a 'triage approach,' " he says. "The problem is that it's difficult for property owners as well as the developers to come in late and find out that the site is significant, protected or being contested. Everyone becomes suspect at that moment. It's far better to be proactive."

Decades in the making

IT'S been 45 years since civic leaders formally recommended that the city take stock of itself. The result was the 1962 Cultural Heritage Ordinance, which allowed individual sites to be designated as historic and/or cultural monuments. One of its key proposals was a need for a comprehensive inventory. But sheer size, timing, money and competing civic concerns — riots, fires, earthquakes — prevented it from being a top priority.

Today, a team of 25 experts — urban historians, academics, architectural historians among them — selected by Jones & Stokes, an environmental and planning consultant firm, have begun preparing a comprehensive "Historic Context Statement," a document that will help shape the survey field guide. (A pilot survey team is set for a test run this year with the formal survey to begin in 2008.) The statement will chart the historic and architectural evolution of L.A., laying out major themes that shaped the city's identity, such as

GLENN KOENIG Los Angeles Times

TAKING A BROADER VIEW: *"We're trying to think not just historically, but, 'What's important to the life of the city?' " says consultant Richard Starzak.*

On the Web

What's your favorite "hidden treasure"? Go to *latimes.com/arts.*

"Hollywood the Place," "Hollywood the Idea" and "Annexation." In addition, it will consider the property types and what makes them important.

"The challenge is really to answer the question: 'Why is a resource significant?' " says Hansen, who is overseeing the project's day-to-day progress. "What are the patterns, the trends, the forces throughout the development history of Los Angeles that made certain property types occur and why?"

Ultimately, Hansen says, the team will develop a narrative that not just details the 150 to 200 property types found around Los Angeles — residential, commercial, industrial and institutional — but will break them into subcategories and clearly define a particular style's characteristics. The Historic Context's section on "Residential Development," for example, would include descriptions of Craftsman architecture, period revival or early public housing along with a list of key features. As well, there will be detailed "eligibility standards" that will lay out criteria for historical designation.

To help contextualize it all, the team Jones & Stokes assembled is conversant in Southern California's vivid, visual language and includes experts in trends including California Bungalow and Googie architecture as well as office buildings of the late 1970s. "There's so much that's happened here, and the traditional way has been to just start chronologically," says the firm's senior architectural historian Richard Starzak. "But there are so many facets of history and people. The biggest challenge is just finding a good starting place. And the city never worked in a line like that. There are just so many layers of culture — fashion, the whole surf-pop culture. And we're trying to think not just historically, but, 'What's important to the life of the city?' What's drawn people? And it's hard to explain that in terms of buildings and structures."

A populist approach

INSPIRED by a New York City-based site, Place Matters, the SurveyL.A. website, still in the works, will offer an opportunity for members of the public to identify their own out-of-plain-sight landmarks. So that could mean pinpointing a nondescript apartment complex or a long-shuttered dance hall with an explanation about why it is noteworthy — architecturally, historically or culturally. "People will be able to talk about sites by answering a series of open-ended questions," says Bernstein, and that information "will be fed into the more formal survey process over the next few years."

The invitation, they realize, could be a Pandora's box, particularly in a city such as Los Angeles where "noteworthy" has a slippery definition. "We will have to provide some cautionary notes along the way," says Bernstein. "The 'George Washington Slept Here' syndrome in Los Angeles may more likely be 'the celebrity lived here' syndrome. That doesn't automatically make a property rise to the level of historic significance."

It's the unearthed surprises, project overseers hope, that will lead to broader implications. And it was that chance to deepen the city's story that George Sanchez found compelling from the beginning. "It's important to create a multiracial baseline to plug into a whole lot of histories that get put on the back burner," says Sanchez, a professor of American studies, ethnicity and history at USC and part of the Jones & Stokes-assembled team. "This way we can start raising issues from the very beginning about how we do this so it isn't just about famous architects and how buildings got built: It's about how space got used," says Sanchez, who is as interested in exploring sites of racial interaction as those that have had multiple meanings over time as neighborhoods evolve — a jewel box of a concert hall known to one generation as a place to hear an orchestra, to another might be known as the union meeting hall.

"One of the things I passed around to the group was a brief history of racial segregation in L.A. Here you have houses that were at the front lines, and through that you can represent the people who were on the front lines. But you don't know that driving by."

The process provides a rare opportunity to think beyond the usual, basic data gathered — when built, who built — says Greg Hise, faculty member in urban history and planning at USC. "So often we are focused on structures but not their stories; not how parts of the city add up as a whole, or how a self-defined neighborhood fits into a larger mosaic."

Trying to sum up something as elusive as L.A., says Hise, "doesn't seem like such a great challenge. It's what scholars do. It's more challenging getting people to ask smart questions that lead us to new answers. How many new stories are we going to be able to bring together — to write this really thick, rich history? Which for a project like this is a very different kind of objective."

lynell.george@latimes.com

Architectural no-brainers

SurveyL.A. is Los Angeles' grand-scale effort to take stock of itself — literally. Organized by the city planning department's Office of Historic Resources, the goal is to identify and catalog Los Angeles' vast built history — more than 800,000 legal parcels. The hope is that it will take us beyond what we think about when we think about Los Angeles — that mishmash of telegenic landmarks, storybook architectural styles and beamed-across-the-globe icons that overtly tell the world a little about ourselves.

GLENN KOENIG Los Angeles Times

HOLLYWOOD BOWL: *Sporting its fifth shell since the 1922 original, the venue has been a stage for countless artists performing under the stars.*

SAM MIRCOVICH Reuters

HOLLYHOCK HOUSE: *Frank Lloyd Wright, in a style he called California Romanza, created high drama along Hollywood Boulevard.*

AL SEIB Los Angeles Times

UNION STATION: *Often the first vision of L.A. for arriving train travelers, the 1939 terminal's color and tiled décor epitomize the Southwest.*

More than meets the eye

What SurveyL.A. hopes to uncover are not just "architectural gems" but the hidden histories behind buildings — especially those not obvious to the naked eye. Beginning in mid-August, the public will be able to assist by going to SurveyL.A.'s soon-to-be-launched website to identify structures that might have played an important role in Los Angeles' complex evolution.

GLENN KOENIG Los Angeles Times

TRINITY AUDITORIUM: *The Los Angeles Philharmonic made its 1919 debut, 11 days after its first rehearsal, in the Grand Avenue structure.*

GLENN KOENIG Los Angeles Times

NAT 'KING' COLE HOME: *The popular singer got a less-than-enthusiastic reception when he moved into all-white Hancock Park.*

In the beginning, a citywide survey for Los Angeles certainly loomed as a daunting challenge. Los Angeles is enormous—a city of 466 square miles and 880,000 separate properties. Public presentations introducing SurveyLA usually began with a map of the Los Angeles boundaries showing outlines of San Francisco, Boston, Cleveland, Milwaukee, Minneapolis, St. Louis, Pittsburgh, and the island of Manhattan fitting inside L.A.'s borders, with plenty of room to spare.

Los Angeles is also a tremendously complex city, with some of the greatest range and diversity of historic resources found anywhere, layers of demographic change, and challenging topography. And at the time, only about 15 percent of the city had ever been surveyed to identify potential historic resources, leaving 85 percent a blank slate for preservation.

But the survey was necessary to move Los Angeles beyond the more reactive, eleventh-hour approach that traditionally defined preservation advocacy. It often seemed like "preservation by triage," as preservation advocates, feeling overwhelmed by the enormity of what needed saving, could only rush to give attention to the most immediately threatened building. For policymakers and Cultural Heritage commissioners, the long absence of a survey in Los Angeles meant piecemeal decision-making, without an ability to anchor their decisions in a fuller understanding of the totality of Los Angeles's historic places.

OHR'S KEN BERNSTEIN AND JANET HANSEN, FEATURED IN A 2007 *LOS ANGELES TIMES* FEATURE ON SURVEYLA, WRITTEN BY LYNELL GEORGE

HOW WAS SURVEYLA CONDUCTED?

SurveyLA was organized around separate surveys of each of the city's thirty-five Community Plan Areas—large geographies that have populations ranging from approximately 50,000 to 300,000 each. This organization reinforced the linkage between the survey and the city's long-range planning: the survey findings were meant to inform and guide the updates of these community plans that define the vision for future growth and land uses in each portion of the city.

OHR divided the thirty-five Community Plan Areas into nine groups of surveys, contracting with historic preservation consulting firms to conduct the field surveys in each group. The consultants on the survey teams were largely trained as architectural historians, with unique expertise in the history and architecture of Los Angeles. The lead consultants were supplemented by interns and volunteers who assisted with research and documentation.

SurveyLA became a very collaborative effort, with multiple professional consulting firms that had previously been competitors, including Architectural Resources Group (ARG), Galvin Preservation Associates (GPA), and Historic Resources Group (HRG) coming together to pool their expertise. The teams began by touring an entire Community Plan Area together, ultimately looking at every street and every property in the city, and came to a collective concurrence on what buildings and

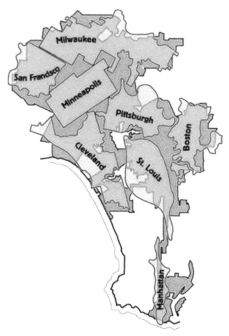

THE LOS ANGELES CITY BOUNDARIES, COMPARED WITH SEVEN MAJOR U.S. CITIES AND THE ISLAND OF MANHATTAN

places appeared to be significant.

Before launching the field surveys, OHR needed to develop the tools and methods necessary to complete a survey in such a large and complex city; in the decades prior to SurveyLA, most historic surveys were completed using pencil, paper, and clipboard. Los Angeles created new technological tools to streamline the survey collection process, becoming the first municipality to complete an all-digital citywide survey at this scale. These included the development of a custom-designed Field Guide Survey System (FIGSS) for use on laptop computers and tablets, which included pre-loaded information that helped inform the survey, such as construction dates, previous survey data, and information gathered from community outreach.

Using the FIGSS on their devices, two-person survey teams could quickly go from property to property in the field: while one team member shot exterior photographs, the other recorded information about the building's architectural features, notable alterations, and significance through a series of drop-down menus.

ENGAGING THE PUBLIC

OHR did significant public outreach six to nine months before sending its survey teams into the field. Outreach focused on eliciting information from community members on places that mattered to them—particularly focused on places of social or cultural significance, which may not have been visually obvious to the survey teams otherwise.

The team used many strategies to spread the word about the survey and seek public input, even beyond traditional community meetings and workshops. Speakers were trained and became part of the SurveyLA Speakers Bureau, serving as volunteer ambassadors for the project and extending the reach of our small staff to become a more regular presence at the city's neighborhood councils, community organizations, and neighborhood events and festivals.

OHR produced a half-hour television program on SurveyLA for the city's cable channel, which was honored with a local Emmy Award. The office also created a social media program as well as a dedicated website ("MyHistoricLA") to "crowd-source" the collection of information on places that mattered to Angelenos.

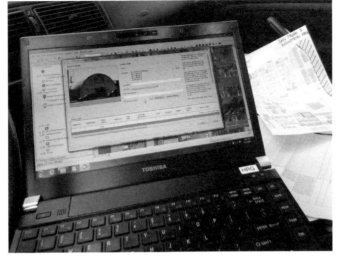

A TYPICAL VEHICLE INTERIOR FOR THE SURVEYLA TEAMS: LAPTOP WITH THE INTERACTIVE FIGSS APPLICATION, ACCOMPANIED BY MAPS AND NOTES (COFFEE AND SNACKS NOT SHOWN)

system, HistoricPlaces-LA (HPLA), which is the city's comprehensive historic resources inventory and management system.

HPLA is now the repository for information on all Los Angeles historic resources. It was the first customization of a system called Arches, which the Getty originally created for its international work, managing information on archaeological resources in the Middle East. HPLA allows users to search for resources in their own communities, view maps, and search by theme or topic.

ACCESSING THE SURVEY

Once the surveys were completed for each area and thoroughly vetted by OHR staff and an expert external Survey Review Committee, summary reports were made available online (Planning4LA.org). To make the survey findings more usable and searchable, GCI again partnered with the city to create a dedicated new

THE IMPACT OF SURVEYLA

As noted previously, the major purpose of the survey is to guide good planning, and particularly to inform long-range plans. To plan thoughtfully for which areas should be protected and which might accommodate more intense development, cities need to know where they might consider avoiding impacts to historic resources, and where they might capitalize on their historic places as community assets.

For example, L.A. City Planning has been using SurveyLA findings to inform the crafting and passage of additional protections against demolitions within "character residential" neighborhoods in West Adams and South Los Angeles that were not yet ready to pursue formal historic district designations. Within these same Community Plan Areas, the comparative absence of significant historic resources in other neighborhoods allowed for plans that create incentives for more intense development near new transit stations.

In Boyle Heights, the survey findings on the neighborhood's predominant architectural styles and features shaped the creation of new zoning tools to promote more compatible new residential development. And in the Sawtelle neighborhood of West Los Angeles, the survey's identification of significant Japanese American cultural heritage is guiding community planning recommendations to preserve and enhance this legacy.

Identification in a survey does not ensure the same level of protection and review that is provided to the landmarked Historic-Cultural Monuments and historic districts described in Chapters 2 and 3. SurveyLA did not formally designate local landmarks or historic districts—it simply identified which places or districts appeared to be "eligible" for designation. In most parts of the city, buildings identified as significant can still be altered or even demolished without further review; day-to-day permits for these properties can generally be issued as before.

Nevertheless, for larger development projects requiring planning and zoning approval that are subject to the State's environmental law (the California

HOME PAGE FROM HISTORICPLACESLA

Environmental Quality Act), the city has been using the survey information to evaluate potential impacts on historic resources. For these larger projects and more significant planning approvals, the survey identification does help ensure that the potential impact on historic resources is publicly disclosed and that possible preservation alternatives are explored.

The survey provides invaluable information for developers and property owners, flagging whether a site under consideration for development may have a significant historic resource. It is far preferable for owners and developers to have this information up front, before investment or development decisions are set in stone, rather than be surprised later by preservation activism seeking to save a site that has architectural or historic significance.

SurveyLA has begun to serve as a model for other major U.S. cities, such as Denver and Philadelphia, which have launched citywide survey initiatives based significantly on SurveyLA's methodology. While it is heartening to have SurveyLA serve as an inspiration for other communities, the experience of Los Angeles mostly underscores what should have been obvious all along: if cities want to take meaningful steps to preserve and enhance significant historic places, they first need to have a comprehensive understanding of what places within their cities are important to preserve.

CHAPTER 4
TELLING L.A.'S DIVERSE STORIES: CREATING PRESERVATION FRAMEWORKS FOR THE CITY'S CULTURAL HISTORY

Los Angeles has become one of the most diverse cities in the nation, with as many as 224 spoken languages and a majority of residents speaking a language other than English in the home. As of 2017, 72 percent of L.A. residents reported a Census Bureau race/ethnicity other than Non-Hispanic/Latino White.

For historic preservation to be relevant and meaningful in Los Angeles, preservation leaders need to ensure that the places they seek to protect fully encompass all of the city's communities and cultures. But how can Angelenos best reach a collective consensus on which places of potential social or cultural significance are worthy of recognition and preservation? And how can community members sharpen their understanding of the forces and places that shaped their own community's unique history and identity within the city?

To help answer such questions, historic preservation professionals have developed a tool called a "historic context statement," which is a comprehensive framework for making historic preservation evaluations.

The city's Office of Historic Resources (OHR) has prepared a series of groundbreaking historic contexts for SurveyLA, addressing Los Angeles's most important ethnic and cultural themes. These frameworks were supported by a series of grants from California's State Office of Historic Preservation. OHR also successfully obtained a National Park Service Underrepresented Communities Grant to prepare the Asian Americans in Los Angeles Context, addressing five of the city's largest Asian American communities.

Because this was the first time that many communities' major historic themes and historic places have been documented through any official governmental initiative, the process of researching and preparing the contexts was just as important as the ultimate written product. OHR and the consultant teams drew upon input from broad public outreach and substantive contributions from local leaders and scholars within each community.

OHR approached this work with the philosophy that

the themes developed through the context documents are not a separate history, but instead need to be seen as fully woven into the larger story of Los Angeles. Each of these specific context documents became part of a citywide framework that guides historic preservation in Los Angeles: SurveyLA's citywide Historic Context Statement. The citywide context represents a comprehensive structure to distill the collective knowledge about Los Angeles's history and architecture, and tie that to places that still exist. Only by understanding how Los Angeles grew and evolved can we begin to evaluate which buildings and places around us today are significant.

SurveyLA's citywide framework is organized around nine major contexts encompassing more than two hundred themes and subthemes, covering topics that range from post-World War II suburbanization to the aerospace industry, Japanese-style gardens to air-raid sirens, and Art Deco architecture to Quonset huts.

This chapter provides some insights into what was found through these efforts: the unique stories and influences that shaped the communities which help define Los Angeles. Each context draws out key themes that give all Angelenos a deeper understanding of how each community contributed to the larger L.A. story. And these themes then connect back to specific places that provide a physical link to each community's contributions to Los Angeles.

Many of the buildings and places identified through these contexts are not the visually stunning showpieces seen in most books on Los Angeles architecture, but instead include modest storefronts or residences of "vernacular" architecture. But whether or not they may have architectural significance, they represent places of deep meaning within the social and cultural histories of their communities. By giving insights into those histories, these contexts shed light on facets of a city that is far richer and more layered than the stereotypical Tinseltown image of Los Angeles.

THE ANNA HOWARD SHAW AND CORA SCOTT POPE RESIDENCE, GARVANZA, A FOCAL POINT FOR THE WOMEN'S SUFFRAGIST MOVEMENT IN THE 1890S.

■ CANDELAS GUITARS, BOYLE HEIGHTS
□ THE EDWARD ROYBAL RESIDENCE, BOYLE HEIGHTS

LATINO LOS ANGELES

Latinos have played an enduring role in the history of Los Angeles, beginning with the city's earliest colonial beginnings; residents of Mexican heritage represented 75 percent of its population in 1850. The Latino Los Angeles Historic Context Statement shows how the Latino presence is deeply embedded in the city's cultural and civic life, yet also reflects a legacy of discrimination. Beginning in neighborhoods near the Plaza at Downtown's El Pueblo, where Los Angeles was founded in 1781, Latino residents dispersed to communities east and south during the early twentieth century. These patterns were shaped by proximity to jobs, the availability of housing, and exclusionary housing policies in many areas of the region.

Commercial Businesses

As the Latino population of Los Angeles began to grow steadily in the post-World War II era, Latino entrepreneurs started opening businesses catering to the burgeoning population. Many of these longer-lasting commercial enterprises, often referred to as "legacy businesses," helped define the cultural character of their communities and remain community anchors to this day.

Candelas Guitars (2724 E. Cesar Chavez Ave., Boyle Heights) is a family business that dates back to 1928 in Torreon, Mexico, and established itself in Boyle Heights in 1947. It is one of the leading makers of guitars for classical, flamenco, and mariachi music, keeping alive traditional music for neighborhood musicians. The Delgado family continues to make their guitars by hand using traditional craftsmanship, and over the decades the store has served prominent performers such as Los Lobos, Pepe Romero, and Jackson Browne.

The Latino Civil Rights Movement

In the 1940s and 1950s, the Latino struggle for equal treatment spurred significant legal challenges to segregation and exclusion, as well as the formation of new community-based organizations—such as the Community Service Organization (CSO), which sought to register Mexican American voters. These efforts led to a series of electoral breakthroughs, with Latino elected officials taking office for the first time in many decades.

The Edward Roybal Residence (628 S. Evergreen Ave., Boyle Heights) offers a tangible link to these advances, spearheaded by an under-recognized political pioneer. In 1949, Roybal was elected as the first Latino to serve on the Los Angeles City Council since 1881. Roybal's presence on the council throughout the 1950s gave the Latino community an important political voice during a period of rapid change. In 1962, Roybal became the first Latino from California elected to the U.S. House of Representatives since 1879. In Congress, where he served for thirty years, he was known as a champion of civil rights and equal access to education, health care, and housing. As an outgrowth of its work on the Latino Los Angeles Historic Context, in 2017 OHR successfully nominated the Roybal Residence for a listing in the National Register of Historic Places, with the full support of its homeowners.

The Struggle for Educational Equity

Despite the 1954 U.S. Supreme Court decision in Brown v. Board of Education, significant school segregation persisted in Los Angeles throughout the 1950s and 1960s. Dramatic disparities in educational outcomes also defined this era, with only 100 Latino students attending UCLA out of an undergraduate student body of 25,000. In the 1960s, increasing Chicano activism focusing on educational equity peaked with the "blow-outs" (or walk-outs) of spring 1968, when more than 15,000 students from several high schools walked out of class to demand smaller classrooms, Latino teachers, Mexican American history classes, and parent advisory boards.

Roosevelt High School (456 S. Mathews St., Boyle Heights) was one of the original five LAUSD high schools involved in the 1968 blow-outs. Opened in 1923, the school was seismically upgraded and remodeled, mostly in the PWA Moderne style, following the 1933 Long Beach earthquake. In 2018, on the fiftieth anniversary of the blow-outs, the L.A. Unified School District approved a plan to demolish most of the culturally significant

ROOSEVELT HIGH SCHOOL, BOYLE HEIGHTS

■ *LOS CUATROS GRANDES*, PAINTED AT ESTRADA COURTS IN 1993 BY ERNESTO DE LA LOZA,
WITH ASSISTANCE FROM LOCAL YOUTH, DEPICTING (FROM LEFT) CESAR CHAVEZ, EMILIANO ZAPATA, PANCHO VILLA, AND CANTINFLAS.
■ CHARLES FELIX, AN ESTRADA COURTS RESIDENT, CURATED THE SITE'S MURAL PROGRAM BEGINNING IN 1973
AND PAINTED SEVERAL MURALS HIMSELF, INCLUDING THIS WORK EVOKING A NORTHWEST COAST TOTEM.

buildings on the property. LAUSD's decisions came despite significant opposition from Roosevelt alumni and significant advocacy led by the Los Angeles Conservancy, and even despite the school's inclusion (along with the other four blow-out schools) on the National Trust for Historic Preservation's list of America's 11 Most Endangered Historic Places.

Latino Visual Arts and the Community Mural Movement

The Los Angeles Latino community has a rich history of public art, influenced beginning in the 1930s by the Mexican muralist movement, most notably identified in Los Angeles with the local work of David Alfaro Siqueiros. During the 1960s and 1970s, the Chicano movement recaptured this connection to muralism, visually

THIS UNTITLED MURAL AT ESTRADA COURTS DEPICTING TWO NATIVE AMERICANS WAS PAINTED
BY A RESIDENT YOUTH NAMED SANDY IN 1974.

depicting its political and social activism through artwork that quickly established Los Angeles as the epicenter for Chicano muralism.

The Estrada Courts Murals (3232 Estrada St., Boyle Heights) are one of the most important examples of public art from this period, located at the Estrada Courts public housing project in Boyle Heights. Several of the works resulted from a partnership between the city's Housing Authority and local Chicano artists, through which neighborhood youth were recruited to produce murals depicting themes related to Chicano heritage and culture, with the guidance of artists. The walls of the buildings eventually displayed more than fifty murals painted by Chicano artists, including Willie Herrón, Charles W. Felix, Wayne Healy, Norma Montoya, and David Botello, as well as Estrada Courts residents who lived there between 1972 and 1978.

The Great Wall of Los Angeles (near 12900 Oxnard St. at Coldwater Canyon Avenue, Valley Glen) is one of the largest murals in the world, stretching 2,754 feet, or more than a half-mile. The mural, painted on the west wall of the Tujunga Flood Control Channel, was completed between 1974 and 1984 by teams of youth, under the supervision of artists led by muralist Judith F. Baca and the Social and Public Art Resource Center (SPARC). Baca's content and design ideas represented an alternative history of California, with scenes emphasizing the role played by Native Americans, Latinos, African Americans, and Asian Americans in creating California's culture, as well as highlighting themes such as immigration, women's rights, racism, and the struggle for gay rights. In 2017, the *Great Wall* was listed in the National Register of Historic Places, through a nomination submitted by the OHR.

■ *THE GREAT WALL OF LOS ANGELES*, VALLEY GLEN

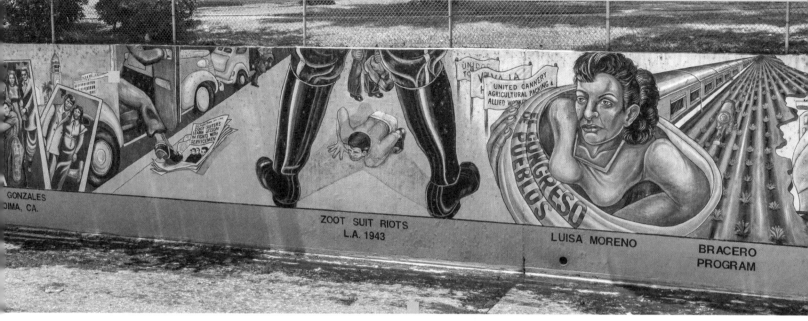

■ *GREAT WALL* DETAIL, DEPICTING IMPORTANT PEOPLE AND EVENTS IN CALIFORNIA LATINO HISTORY, INCLUDING LABOR ACTIVIST LUISA MORENO, PACOIMA WORLD WAR II HERO DAVID GONZALES, AND THE 1943 ZOOT SUIT RIOTS
■ *THE GREAT WALL OF LOS ANGELES*, WITH CREDITS TO MANY OF THE MURAL'S COMMUNITY-BASED ARTISTIC CONTRIBUTORS

AFRICAN AMERICANS IN LOS ANGELES

The African Americans in Los Angeles Historic Context document illuminated the places associated with the city's African American community, which played a central role in the political, social, cultural, and artistic development of Los Angeles despite pervasive racial discrimination. The African American story in Los Angeles includes: sites associated with segregation and discrimination; commercial establishments that catered to African Americans in a segregated era; newspapers and publications that shaped African American culture; places associated with political leaders and institutions that led the fight for civil rights and economic progress; and sites that reflect the community's prominent contributions to music, art, and entertainment.

Deed Restrictions and Racial Segregation

For the first half of the twentieth century, African Americans were generally prohibited from living west of Main Street, extending from Downtown south to Watts. Restrictive covenants—legal clauses written into deeds specifying that owners could only sell their property to "Caucasians"—were one of the most pervasive tools to reinforce residential segregation. The federal government's Home Owners Loan Corporation (HOLC) reinforced this separation through its lending practices. The HOLC established an appraisal system for its low-interest loans, rating neighborhoods as "security risks" based upon a largely racially determined ranking. African American, Mexican American, and Asian

THE HOME OWNERS LOAN CORPORATION (HOLC) "REDLINING" MAP OF LOS ANGELES, 1939

■ HATTIE MCDANIEL RESIDENCE, 2203 S. HARVARD BLVD. IN THE SUGAR HILL NEIGHBORHOOD OF WEST ADAMS
■ LINCOLN HOTEL, DOWNTOWN LOS ANGELES

American neighborhoods were relegated to the lowest rating, depicted on maps with a red color, originating the term "redlining."

The Sugar Hill neighborhood (West Adams Heights), identified as an eligible historic district in SurveyLA, contains twenty-five properties bounded by 22nd and 25th Streets and Harvard and Hobart Boulevards. The neighborhood is significant for its association with African Americans' quest to end deed restrictions that promoted racial segregation. Here in 1945, black homeowners—including actresses Louise Beavers, Hattie McDaniel, and Ethel Waters—hired attorney Loren Miller to defend the right to own property and live in this once all-white neighborhood. Miller's successful legal action led him to take the issue of restrictive covenants to the U.S. Supreme Court, which, in *Shelley v. Kramer* (1948), ruled that racially restrictive deed restrictions were unenforceable.

Commercial Development

Black-owned businesses were a source of community pride and economic success, providing retail services, restaurants, and local goods to African American neighborhoods. Over the decades, prominent businesses such as Golden State Mutual Life Insurance Company, Broadway Federal Savings and Loan, and Angelus Funeral Home became important institutions in the community. *The Negro Motorist Green Book*, created by Victor H. Green in 1936, became a necessary guide for African Americans' road trips during a time of Jim Crow segregation. In Los Angeles, the 1956 edition of *The Green Book*, as it came to be known, included twenty-seven businesses, most of which no longer remain.

The Lincoln Hotel (549 Ceres Ave., Downtown Los Angeles), constructed in 1916, is significant as a long-time establishment for African American travelers; it was included in *The Green Book* continuously between 1939 and 1961. In 2001, the hotel, located just east of the heart of Skid Row, was converted to forty-one affordable efficiency apartments by the non-profit developer Skid Row Housing Trust.

Newspapers and Publications

Local newspapers helped ground the African American community's local identity, providing information and social connection. They helped support black-owned businesses, publicized local social events, and advocated for civil rights. The two most significant black

newspapers were the *California Eagle* and the *Los Angeles Sentinel*, both of which made a significant impact over many decades.

Joseph and Charlotta Bass House (697 E. 52nd Pl., Southeast Los Angeles) was the residence of the Basses, who were co-editors and publishers of the *California Eagle*, a prominent African American newspaper in Los Angeles that ran from 1879 to 1964. Joseph died in the 1930s, and Charlotta continued to manage the newspaper for nearly two more decades before selling the publication to Loren Miller in 1952 and devoting her later years to politics. The Basses lived in this house from 1930 to 1945. It is listed in the National and California Registers as a contributing structure to the Fifty-Second Place Historic District, which is also an HPOZ.

Civil Rights and Political Advancement

The Los Angeles African American community began to achieve more substantial political representation in 1963 with the election of three African American city council members: Gilbert Lindsay, Billy Mills, and Tom Bradley. These elections, as well as other successful candidacies in state legislative and federal congressional

races, paved the way for Bradley's election in 1973 as the city's first African American mayor.

Mayor Tom Bradley's house (3807 S. Welland Ave., Leimert Park) is the most significant physical link to Los Angeles's longest-serving mayor, who served a twenty-year tenure (1973 to 1993). Bradley lived in this house when he was elected to the Los Angeles City Council in 1963, and the home served as a base for his early political campaigns. His mayoral administration not only led the expansion of the Downtown Los Angeles skyline and brought the 1984 Olympic Games to the city, but also significantly advanced civil rights, opening the doors of city government to new African American, Asian, and Latino leaders.

Women's Clubs

Beginning in the early twentieth century, Los Angeles developed a strong network of women's clubs. By 1910, there were approximately twenty black women's clubs across the city, mostly under the umbrella of the California Association of Colored Women's Clubs (CWC). Many of the clubs promoted an ethos of motherhood and traditional morality, while advancing political activism around civil rights.

Wilfandel Club (3425 W. Adams Blvd.) was founded

■ WILFANDEL CLUB, WEST ADAMS
■ WILFANDEL CLUB INTERIOR

in 1945 within the West Adams community to promote civic betterment and culture. The Wilfandel Club took its name from a portmanteau of the names of its primary founders, Della Williams and Fannie Williams. Club members raised funds to purchase this property that was once the home of real estate developer Percy Clark. The clubhouse was one of the few integrated public meeting spaces in Los Angeles during the 1940s and 1950s, and is still used today as a site for weddings, social gatherings, and events.

Los Angeles's Jazz Scene

Jazz helped put L.A.'s African American community on the map nationally and internationally. Among the early jazz musicians who moved to Los Angeles from New Orleans were Edward "Kid" Ory, Paul Howard, and Jelly Roll Morton. The main jazz nightclubs—including Club Alabam, The Downbeat, The Flame, and The Casablanca—were concentrated along Central Avenue in Southeast Los Angeles. The Central Avenue jazz scene peaked in the 1930s and declined by the 1950s, when integrated clubs opened elsewhere and the African American community began to settle further west within the city.

Jack's Basket Room (3217 S. Central Ave.) was once one of the street's popular jazz clubs, though its name frequently changed during its years of operation (1939 to 1951). When the historic context work for SurveyLA was completed in early 2018, the clubs were gone, but this building still stood. Then in March 2018, with no public notice, the building was suddenly demolished after being red-tagged by the Department of Building and Safety due to fire damage.

CENTRAL AVENUE'S CLUB ALABAM, CIRCA 1945

JEWISH LOS ANGELES

With a Jewish population second only to New York City's for many decades, Los Angeles has one of the most vibrant Jewish communities in the nation. From the 1920s through the 1940s, there were two major centers of the Los Angeles Jewish population: Boyle Heights, which largely attracted recent immigrants from Eastern Europe, and Mid-Wilshire/Hollywood/West Adams, where middle-class and affluent Jewish professionals settled. During the post-World War II years, the Jewish community moved west and north, to the Westside and San Fernando Valley communities.

The Jewish History Context for SurveyLA captures the richness of Jewish religion and spirituality and the social clubs and organizations that created community cohesion, as well as Jewish contributions to health and medicine, commercial business, and L.A.'s entertainment industry.

THE FORMER AGUDATH ACHIM CONGREGATION, WEST ADAMS

Religious Institutions

From the 1850s frontier to the suburbs of more recent decades, Jewish religious practice in Los Angeles has focused on establishing and maintaining Jewish community identity through traditional cultural and spiritual values. Synagogues became centers of community and neighborhood fixtures as Los Angeles Jews spread into neighborhoods beyond downtown. By the 1920s and 1930s, numerous new synagogues were being constructed, often in historicist styles that reflected the legacies of ancient or centuries-old Jewish communities.

Agudath Achim Congregation (2521 W. View St.), a synagogue constructed in 1936 within the South Los Angeles/West Adams neighborhood, reflects the westward movement of a congregation that began on the eastern edge of Downtown, at Twenty-First Street and Central Avenue, in 1908. The congregation occupied the building until 1957, when the Jewish community continued to move westward. Metropolitan AME Zion, a prominent African American congregation, acquired the property and occupied the building for nearly sixty years.

Commercial Businesses

Many Jewish entrepreneurs established businesses that made important contributions to the development of the Jewish community and often became beloved neighborhood landmarks, fostering the distinctively Jewish social and cultural history of the city. Many of these Jewish businesses began in Boyle Heights in the 1920s, 1930s, and 1940s. But later, a significant Jewish commercial center developed during the 1940s and 1950s in the Fairfax District between Wilshire Boulevard and Melrose Avenue, with a high concentration of kosher butcher shops, bakeries, and religious music and book stores.

■ CANTER'S DELI, ORIGINAL BOYLE HEIGHTS LOCATION, 1939
■ CANTER'S DELI, FAIRFAX

Canter's Deli (2323 E. Cesar Chavez Ave., formerly Brooklyn Avenue, in Boyle Heights and 419 N. Fairfax Ave) strongly reflects the Jewish community's identity in both Boyle Heights and the Fairfax District. The Canter Brothers Delicatessen, which originated in Jersey City in 1924, went out of business following the stock market crash in 1929. The three Canter brothers decided to head west for California and found a new location in the Boyle Heights neighborhood, opening a deli on Brooklyn Avenue (now Cesar Chavez Avenue) in 1931. Their original location remained in business until the 1970s, and they opened a second location at 439 N. Fairfax Ave. in 1948. In 1953, they moved up the street to acquire and convert the Esquire Theater at 419 North Fairfax Ave., where the deli remains today.

Jewish Political and Labor Institutions

Jewish leaders played a significant role in the Los Angeles labor movement for many decades. In the early years of Jewish settlement, the Labor Zionist movement advocated for Yiddish-based cultural nationalism and socialism, as well as for a Jewish state in Palestine.

Vladeck Center (126 N. St. Louis St., Boyle Heights) was named for Baruch Charney Vladeck, a prominent Jewish labor leader, politician, and journalist. The Vladeck Center served as a meeting venue for local Jewish labor organizations and was considered the secular heart of Jewish life in Boyle Heights between 1941 and 1960, as well as a touchpoint between the Jewish community in Boyle Heights and the rapidly growing Latino community. The building was slated for demolition in 2006, to prepare for the construction of a new Hollenbeck Police Station. However, a coalition of Jewish and Latino community members, with the assistance of the Los Angeles Conservancy, successfully advocated for the building's preservation and reuse as part of the police facility.

Entertainment Industry

The emergence of Hollywood as the center of motion pictures, and then of music, radio, and television, was tied to several waves of first- and second-generation Jewish immigrants from Central and Eastern Europe. A new Jewish elite emerged during these early years, including film moguls such as Samuel Goldwyn, Carl Laemmle, Jesse Lasky, Louis B. Mayer, Adolph Zukor,

and Irving Thalberg. These moguls' own working-class immigrant roots gave them an instinctive connection to their mass audiences, while their eagerness to assimilate led them to manufacture a homogenized on-screen vision of the American Dream—an ethos that significantly shaped the growth of the entertainment industry, and in the process transformed Los Angeles.

The Louis B. Mayer Beach House (144 N. Ocean Way) was the Pacific Palisades retreat for the mogul who established the Metro Film Corporation in 1916 and worked with Marcus Loew to merge Metro with Goldwyn Pictures Corporation in 1924. The resulting MGM would become the biggest studio in Hollywood, famous for its lavish, colorful musicals. Because Mayer's Bel-Air house was demolished, his beach house appears to be the only residence associated with his life during his productive career as a studio mogul.

■ VLADECK CENTER, BOYLE HEIGHTS
■ LOUIS B. MAYER BEACH HOUSE, PACIFIC PALISADES

LGBT LOS ANGELES

SurveyLA's Lesbian, Gay, Bisexual, and Transgender (LGBT) Historic Context, released in 2014, was the first LGBT context prepared for any large U.S. municipality, serving as a model for other cities. The context's introduction advances this key premise:

> Los Angeles has led the nation in cultivating a politicized gay consciousness and building gay institutions. The city's prominent role in creating the modern gay political movement, however, has been overshadowed by the symbolic power of New York's Stonewall riots in 1969 as well as San Francisco's reputation as the country's preeminent gay city.

A 1967 EDITION OF *THE ADVOCATE* NEWSPAPER

was needed to challenge anti-gay discrimination.

Harry Hay House (2328 Cove Ave., Silver Lake) was the home of Harry Hay (1912–2002), an actor, political activist, and early leader in the formation and growth of the Mattachine Society. At this location on November 11, 1950, a group of gay men held the first meeting of what became the Mattachine Society. Hay was forced to abandon leadership of the society during the Red Scare in 1953, due to his connections to the Communist Party. However, the Society subsequently became influential in multiple locations around the nation. This location is now commemorated by the City of Los Angeles, which renamed the adjacent Cove Avenue public staircase the "Mattachine Steps."

The Gay Liberation Movement

Los Angeles's activism in the gay liberation movement can be divided into two phases: a period of consciousness raising, followed by a period focused on political organizing. Arguably, the most significant event launching the gay liberation movement was the founding of the Mattachine Society in 1950, which took its name from a group of medieval dancers who appeared only in mask. The group argued that homosexuality was not merely a sexual orientation but, rather, a minority group with a unique culture (like Blacks, Latinos, and Jews), and that a grassroots movement of gay people

HARRY HAY HOUSE, SILVER LAKE

BETH CHAYIM CHADASHIM, MID-CITY

Reconciliation of Homosexuality and Religion

At a time when organized religious groups typically condemned or barred LGBT persons on the basis of their sexuality and identity, Los Angeles was at the forefront of change in these practices, through the efforts of key religious leaders and institutions beginning in the 1950s. L.A. has also been home to some of the earliest LGBT-friendly religious institutions in the nation.

Beth Chayim Chadashim (6000 W. Pico Blvd., Mid-City) was the first gay and lesbian synagogue in the world. Formed in 1973, the congregation originally made its home in Leo Baeck Temple before establishing the Pico location in 1977. After applying for membership in the Union of American Hebrew Congregations (known today as the Union for Reform Judaism) in 1973—stirring a heated debate among the rabbis—it became the first gay congregation of any denomination to be recognized by its religious group's larger governing body.

Gay Bars as Social Institutions

Los Angeles has a significant legacy of gay bars, which played an important role as some of the few places where LGBT persons could be themselves in public. Some of the earliest gay bars were on Bunker Hill and near Pershing Square in Downtown, but by the 1930s many had opened along the Sunset Strip (in today's West Hollywood) and in Westlake, Hollywood, and North Hollywood. These bars were also places where people became engaged politically, as demonstrated by the 1967 protest following the police raid at the Black Cat Bar in Silver Lake.

Jewel's Catch One (4076 W. Pico Blvd., Mid-City), reportedly the first LGBT African American disco in the nation, opened in 1973. The club filled an important void in the community by providing a welcoming space for all, including Black lesbian and transgender individuals. Its owner, Jewel Thais-Williams, opened a medical clinic adjacent to the club to provide care for disenfranchised LGBT/African American patients, becoming an important non-profit medical institution during the AIDS epidemic of the 1980s and 1990s. Thais-Williams sold the club in 2015, and in 2016 it reopened as the Union, "the last Black-owned disco," before reverting to the Catch One name more recently.

JEWEL'S CATCH ONE, MID-CITY

ISHERWOOD-BACHARDY RESIDENCE, SANTA MONICA CANYON
LIVING ROOM OF ISHERWOOD-BACHARDY RESIDENCE; DAVID HOCKNEY'S ICONIC 1968 DOUBLE PORTRAIT PAINTING OF ISHERWOOD AND BACHARDY DEPICTS THEM IN THIS ROOM'S WICKER CHAIRS

The LGBT Community and Media

In the mid-twentieth century, magazines, newspapers, and newsletters became a source of valuable information for LGBT communities, offering social networking, legal advice, and visibility for local businesses. Many of the most influential national publications originated in Los Angeles, including the earliest known example of an LGBT magazine in America: *Vice Versa*, originally created at Hollywood's RKO Studios by Edith Eyde, a secretary on the studio lot.

The Advocate (863 N. Virgil Ave., Silver Lake) was a newspaper founded in 1967, soon after the police raid at the nearby Black Cat Bar. The publication began as a small newsletter for a local gay rights group, Personal Rights in Defense and Education (PRIDE), and began national distribution in 1969. It remains the longest-running LGBT publication in print.

Gays and Lesbians in the L.A. Literary Scene

For many decades, some of the most important writers whose work addressed LGBT themes lived in Los Angeles. These included Thomas Mann, Gore Vidal, Christopher Isherwood, John Rechy, and Patricia Nell Warren.

Mann emigrated from Nazi Germany in 1933 and settled in Pacific Palisades two decades after writing *Death in Venice* (1912), one of the first mainstream novels to address same-sex attraction. His later works had homoerotic overtones as well, including *Confessions of Felix Krull: Confidence Man* (1954). Rechy became known in the 1960s for his semi-autobiographical novels *City of Night* (1963) and *This Day's Death* (1969); the latter tells the story of a young man on trial for prostitution in Griffith Park.

Christopher Isherwood Residence (145 Adelaide Dr., Santa Monica Canyon) was home to the acclaimed author and his partner, artist Don Bachardy, for thirty years (1956–1986). Isherwood was an English novelist who moved to Los Angeles during World War II. His short story "Sally Bowles" was inspired by his time in Berlin from 1930 to 1933 and later adapted into the stage and film musical *Cabaret*. His celebrated novel *A Single Man* (1964) depicts a day in the life of a gay, middle-aged Englishman who is a professor at a Los Angeles university, and was adapted in 2009 for a film directed by Tom Ford.

ASIAN AMERICANS IN LOS ANGELES

Each of the contexts for the city's five largest Asian American communities—the Japanese American, Chinese American, Korean American, Thai American, and Filipino American communities:

> ...Discusses the dynamic waves of immigration and settlement patterns of Asian Americans in Los Angeles. Within each group, the power of place resonates as Asian Americans find places of residence, work, and community as Angelenos. With a long history of discrimination, displacement, and associated demolition of property, Asian Americans resisted and struggled to maintain a sense of identity, as well as their homes, businesses, and cultural institutions. (Michelle G. Magalong, Ph.D. and David K. Yoo, Ph.D., Preface to Asian Americans in Los Angeles Contexts)

JAPANESE AMERICAN CONTEXT

Since 1910, Los Angeles has been home to the largest population of Japanese Americans on the U.S. mainland. The Issei (first generation immigrants) shaped numerous local industries, including fishing, canning, gardening, and agriculture, and established Little Tokyo, the largest Japantown in the nation. L.A.'s Japanese Americans created a rich network of social, cultural, and religious institutions that were then obliterated when the community was relocated and detained in internment camps during World War II. Issei and Nisei (the second generation) returned to Los Angeles after the war and established new communities in multiple neighborhoods around the city, contributing to the multi-cultural identity of Los Angeles.

Japanese Settlement in Los Angeles

While Little Tokyo was always Los Angeles's primary Japantown, SurveyLA highlighted important settlements of Japanese Americans in other areas of the city. Sawtelle in West Los Angeles was the westernmost Japanese American enclave in L.A., predating Sawtelle's consolidation into the City of Los Angeles in 1922. Japanese Americans initially came to the area to work in the agricultural fields south of Pico Boulevard, or at the nearby Soldier's Home. The Sawtelle community remains a vibrant center of Japanese American businesses and institutions today.

Yamaguchi Bonsai Nursery (1903 S. Sawtelle Blvd., West Los Angeles), is one of several long-standing local businesses associated with the Japanese American community in Sawtelle. Yamaguchi Bonsai Nursery opened in 1934, and by 1941 Sawtelle had twenty-six Japanese American nurseries serving the growing nearby affluent communities of the Westside, as well

YAMAGUCHI BONSAI NURSERY, SAWTELLE/WEST LOS ANGELES

PRESERVATION PROFILE:
KRISTEN HAYASHI

Kristen Hayashi oversees the permanent collection of the Japanese American National Museum, following nearly a decade in research and collections at the Natural History Museum of Los Angeles County. While pursuing her Ph.D. in history and public history at UC Riverside, she turned to preservation advocacy for sites significant to the Japanese American community. She led the successful effort to designate the Japanese Hospital in Boyle Heights as a Historic-Cultural Monument, and later also prepared the successful HCM nomination for the Tokio Florist/Sakai Residence in Silver Lake.

I developed an interest in history from a fairly young age. Both of my parents were teachers, so every summer we would go on educational family trips. When I was in grad school, I was at the "L.A. as Subject" Archives Bazaar where I saw a table for the Little Tokyo Historical Society. I asked them if there was a project where they needed some help, and they said, "Yes, actually, there's this Japanese Hospital that has an amazing history and we'd like to have it declared a historic landmark, but we just don't know how to start."

What's so beautiful about the Japanese Hospital is that it's a civil rights victory all Angelenos can be proud of. Five Japanese immigrants wanted to improve their community by building a hospital at a time when immigrants were turned away from getting health care. They applied for incorporation in 1926 and were denied by the California Secretary of State, since the Alien Land Law prohibited immigrants who were not eligible for citizenship from owning land. These five immigrant doctors bravely said they were going to fight this, and both the California and the U.S. Supreme Courts ruled in their favor in 1928; in 1929, they were able to raise enough money to build this hospital for the community.

In December 2019, we celebrated the hospital's ninetieth anniversary with a big community birthday party. Among the hundred people there, I'd say two-thirds of them had a personal connection to the hospital, and as they shared their anecdotes, it just felt so much like community. It's been incredibly meaningful to do this work. I felt like I was making a difference in broadening our understanding of Los Angeles's diverse past by preserving this one important story.

I still feel we have a great challenge ahead because so many of the buildings that are significant to our community aren't necessarily known for architecture, but for the purpose they served. It's more of the seemingly mundane sites that should be designated. I'm thinking of places like Fukui Mortuary: it's in a very ordinary building, but the impact it's had in the community has been huge. Or places like Fugetsu-Do, which is a longtime Japanese confectionery in Little Tokyo. And how does preservation help us to preserve intangible cultural heritage—traditions like the Nisei Week parade or New Year's festivals?

Japanese Americans have made huge contributions to Los Angeles history since the 1880s, and I don't think these stories are as well-known as they should be. Our work is cut out for us since there's still a huge discrepancy in terms of how many Historic-Cultural Monuments reflect those stories. The work of SurveyLA has been so important in helping to identify potential sites and in telling the community, "Your history matters." Hopefully it will help community members take the next step to write nominations. It's a huge first step for the City of L.A. to acknowledge that these places and buildings have historical significance. ✶

SEINAN JUDO DOJO/SEINAN KENDO DOJO, SOUTH LOS ANGELES

as Japanese American gardeners who worked in these neighborhoods. The nurseries also served as an anchor for a significant Japanese American business district that had begun to grow in Sawtelle by the 1930s.

Sports and Recreation

In addition to baseball, traditional Japanese sports and martial arts were popular in the local Japanese American community. Judo clubs became common in Southern California, and tournaments were held regularly in Little Tokyo. Dojos (training facilities for martial arts) began to appear in several Los Angeles Japanese American communities.

Seinan Judo Dojo/Seinan Kendo Dojo (1442 W. 36th Pl., South Los Angeles) is the former location of the Seinan Dojo, a significant Judo and Kendo Dojo known for the legendary Japanese American teachers who taught there in the years before and after World War II. The lessons were held in a single-family home, within a neighborhood that was also anchored by two Japanese American institutions on the same block, Senshin Buddhist Temple and Senshin Gakuin (a language school).

CHINESE AMERICAN CONTEXT

While Los Angeles's Chinese Americans were concentrated around the Los Angeles Plaza at El Pueblo—the original city settlement—virtually nothing remains of this original Chinatown, since it was razed for the construction of Los Angeles Union Station in the 1930s. Little also remains of a second settlement in the area historically called City Market in the southern portion of Downtown, which is associated with Chinese American entrepreneurship in truck farming and the produce industry. The Chinese American context for SurveyLA revealed many significant places associated with the later Chinatown, opened beginning in 1938, and with later Chinese American settlement throughout other areas of the city.

The New Chinatown Development

In response to the destruction of Old Chinatown for the construction of Union Station, businessman and community leader Peter Soo Hoo Sr. joined other Chinese

RESTORED Y.C. HONG OFFICE BUILDING INTERIOR, CHINATOWN

business owners in 1937 to create the Los Angeles Chinatown Project Association (later renamed the Los Angeles Chinatown Corporation). Architects Erle Webster and Adrian Wilson designed some of the most elaborate buildings on Chinatown's Central Plaza, incorporating architectural details of Asian architecture and painting the buildings in bright colors, topped with clay tile roofs.

The Y.C. Hong Office Building (445 W. Gin Ling Way, Chinatown), constructed in 1938, is a particularly notable building within Central Plaza for its association with You Chung (Y.C.) Hong, the first Chinese American to pass the California State Bar and practice law in Los Angeles. Hong was a major property owner in Central Plaza and became a prominent immigration lawyer, working for more than fifty years to protect the civil rights of Chinese Americans seeking to become American citizens. He served for nearly a quarter century as the local and national leader of the Chinese American Citizens Alliance (CACA). The second floor of the building served as Hong's office until his death in 1977. Hong had hired a female interior designer, Honor Easton, who designed the office, furniture, and light fixtures using the vernacular of Chinese imagery. The office was restored in 2006 by its new owner, architect Richard Liu, to the way it looked in 1938.

Chinese American Architects in Los Angeles

In the years after World War II, an increasing number of Asian American architects attended local universities such as USC, became members of the American Institute of Architects, worked with well-known firms, and then opened their own firms. Many Asian American architects from this period designed buildings in the Mid-Century Modern style, as well as the Asian Eclectic

CHOY RESIDENCE, SILVER LAKE

style. The ongoing growth of Chinatown in the postwar period provided opportunities for Chinese American architects, among which the work of Eugene Choy, Gilbert Leong, and Gin Wong is perhaps best known.

Choy Residence (3027 Castle St., Silver Lake), built in 1949, is a notable work of Chinese American architect Eugene Choy, designed in the Mid-Century Modern style with extensive redwood siding. Choy emigrated from China with his family at age eleven, received his architectural training at the USC School of Architecture, and founded the Choy Associates architectural firm in 1947, which continues to operate, now under the direction of Choy's son, Barton. Eugene was only the second Chinese American architect to be admitted to the American Institute of Architects (AIA), after I.M. Pei. Choy's residential designs are concentrated in the Silver Lake neighborhood.

KOREAN AMERICAN CONTEXT

Los Angeles has one of the largest Korean populations outside of the Korean peninsula, with a dynamic and long-expanding Koreatown that has served as home to hundreds of Korean American-owned small businesses, churches, and community institutions. Although L.A.'s Korean American community was small prior to the relaxation of federal immigration restrictions in 1965, an important early Korean American community dates from 1903, when laborers arrived in Los Angeles from Hawaii. This early settlement was anchored by two historic sites sharing the same campus on Jefferson Boulevard, near USC: the Korean Presbyterian Church of Los Angeles (1906), which is among the oldest Korean American congregations in the nation; and the building that housed the Korean National Association (1938), which played a key role in supporting Korean independence from Japan. The 1992 civil unrest represented a turbulent chapter for L.A.'s Korean American community, and in subsequent decades, Korean Americans have continued to settle across the region.

THE KOREATOWN DEVELOPMENT ASSOCIATION BUILDING, KOREATOWN

Korean American Civil Rights

In the years following World War II, the Korean American community of Los Angeles had only about 800 residents. Several court cases in the late 1940s and early 1950s challenged discriminatory racial covenant laws that barred Asian Americans from living in certain neighborhoods. Lawsuits brought by two Asian Americans in Los Angeles, Tommy Amer of Chinese heritage and Yin Kim of Korean heritage, were among the legal cases that helped end housing segregation, which allowed the nucleus of Korean American settlement to expand north and west toward present-day Koreatown.

The Yin Kim Residence (1201 S. Gramercy Pl., Country Club Park) was the home of a second-generation Korean-American and U.S. Army veteran, who purchased the house in present-day Country Club Park despite racially restrictive covenants. Kim and his wife quietly moved in during escrow to avoid an injunction that would have prevented them from occupying the

YIN KIM RESIDENCE, COUNTRY CLUB PARK

property. Once the sale closed and they were served the injunction, they challenged it in court, but remained in the house while the case proceeded. The U.S. Supreme Court accepted Amer's case and Kim's case as examples of how restrictive covenants affected other non-white groups in addition to African Americans. In Yin·Kim v. Superior Court (1948), the Supreme Court vacated the injunction, allowing the Kims to continue living in the neighborhood.

The Growth of Koreatown

The catalyst for the formation of Koreatown is often attributed to the 1969 opening of the Olympic Market by Hi Duk Lee, at 3122 W. Olympic Blvd. The success of the market led Lee to open the VIP Palace restaurant (Young Bin Kwan) at 3014 W. Olympic Blvd. in 1975. By 1977, the neighborhood had more than 70,000 Korean American residents and more than fifty Korean restaurants.

The Koreatown Development Association (981 S. Western Ave., Koreatown) was the physical headquarters for the effort to create and promote an emerging Koreatown. The KDA worked at this location as a booster organization for the burgeoning Korean American community, promoting cultural events as well as commerce. It established the Korean Street Festival in 1974, which quickly grew to include over 120 participating organizations with over 45,000 attendees. In 1978, the neighborhood received its honorary recognition as Koreatown by the City of Los Angeles, after lobbying by the KDA, led by its president, Hi Duk Lee. This four-story Modern office building that housed the KDA had been purchased in 1975 by the Korean Association of Southern California (known today as the Korean American Federation) and also housed several other Korean American community organizations.

FILIPINO AMERICAN CONTEXT

The Filipino Americans in Los Angeles Historic Context traces the evolution of a significant community with a history in the city dating back to 1903. Downtown's Little Manila, the core of which was adjacent to the heart of Little Tokyo, became a center of Filipino cultural and commercial activity from the 1920s through the 1940s, but by the 1950s most of it had been destroyed by city-sponsored redevelopment programs. Following World War II, two new concentrations of Los Angeles Filipino life developed. Many Filipino servicemen were drawn back to the harbor communities of Wilmington and San Pedro, which had a strong military presence. During the same period, Filipino-serving churches relocated to the Temple-Beverly neighborhood, helping establish an area that ultimately became officially designated by the city as Historic Filipinotown in 2002.

Community Centers

During the postwar years, the Temple-Beverly neighborhood provided available housing and two Filipino community touchstones: St. Columban Catholic Church,

THE FILIPINO AMERICAN COMMUNITY OF LOS ANGELES/ FILIPINO AMERICAN CULTURAL CENTER, HISTORIC FILIPINOTOWN

and the Filipino Christian Church (HCM #651), which was successfully nominated to the National Register of Historic Places in 2018 by the Office of Historic Resources. Filipino entrepreneurs opened restaurants, neighborhood markets, and barbershops that became community gathering places, such as Morong Café (now Little Ongpin) at 1700 Beverly Blvd. and Luzon Plaza, a shopping center at 1925 W. Temple St., created to serve the Filipino community.

The Filipino American Community of Los Angeles/ Filipino American Cultural Center (1740 W. Temple St.) is considered the heart of today's Historic Filipinotown. The Filipino American Community of Los Angeles (FACLA) was originally established in 1945 as a halfway house for Filipino farmworkers, making it one of the earliest civic groups to serve the Filipino immigrant community. Following extensive fundraising within the Filipino community, the current building (named the Filipino American Cultural Center) was constructed as a social hall in 1965. Its opening represented a significant institutional milestone for the Filipino American community in the area, and FACLA's building has been an important hub ever since for activities such as dances, celebrations, and community meetings.

The Tiki-Ti Bar (4427 Sunset Blvd., East Hollywood/Silver Lake) was established and opened in 1961 by Filipino American Ray Buhen, who was born in the Philippines in 1909 and immigrated to Los Angeles in 1930. Buhen worked as a bartender for many years in other Polynesian-themed bars, including Don the Beachcomber, where he was part of a citywide cadre of Filipino waiters, bartenders, and busboys who played a key role in popularizing tropical drinks. The Tiki-Ti has become an iconic Los Angeles bar over many decades, with classic drinks created by Buhen that are still served

THE TIKI-TI BAR, EAST HOLLYWOOD/SILVER LAKE

today. The establishment is owned and operated by Ray's son and grandson, who lead patrons every Wednesday night in a toast to Ray Buhen and his contributions to the community.

THAI AMERICAN CONTEXT

The Thai community has a shorter Los Angeles history than the other Asian American communities, arriving in the city starting in the 1950s. Thai community settlement in Los Angeles was closely identified with food, notably with early Thai restaurants that date to the 1970s. These eateries reinvented Thai cuisine in various ways to meet the rising demand for Thai food around Los Angeles. Significant new institutions such as the Thai Community Development Center and Wat Thai emerged to meet the needs of a rapidly changing community.

Religious Institutions in the Thai Community

In 1970, a small group of Thai students formed a committee to establish a *wat* (place of worship) to meet the spiritual needs of the growing Thai community in Los Angeles. The Theravada Buddhist Center, Inc. unofficially became the first Thai Buddhist temple in the U.S. in 1971, offering services in a suburban home in today's North Hills community. In the same year, a mission of Thai monks arrived in Los Angeles and worked with members of the Thai community to raise funds to purchase 2.2 acres in Sun Valley for a new temple. Meanwhile, many Thai Christians living in or near Hollywood attended the Hollywood Seventh-Day Adventist Church at 1711 N. Van Ness Ave.

Wat Thai Temple (8225 Coldwater Canyon Blvd., Sun Valley) was completed and dedicated in 1979 as the largest Thai Theravada Buddhist temple in the U.S.

Since its opening, the Wat Thai of Los Angeles has remained the center of spiritual, social, and cultural life for Los Angeles's Thai community, attracting thousands of Thai and non-Thai visitors each year. The temple complex includes a library, a Buddhist Sunday school, and living quarters, or *kuti*, for monks and nuns living on-site. The temple has also operated an outdoor food court within its parking lot. The construction of the Wat Thai of Los Angeles was also a catalyst for growth of Thai businesses along Sherman Way in North Hollywood.

Strengthening Community Identity Through Food

The Thai community's settlement patterns were closely tied to locations near Thai businesses and restaurants, particularly the early Thai restaurants of East Hollywood. Many Thai restaurants were family-operated businesses, with proprietors serving family recipes and often employing other Thais as kitchen and wait staff, providing a significant source of employment for the community. By the late 1970s, one-third of all Thai-owned businesses were restaurants.

Chao Krung Restaurant (111 N. Fairfax Ave., Beverly Fairfax) is one of the few Thai restaurants from the earliest period of community development in the 1970s to remain in continuous operation. Originally located at 5529 Hollywood Boulevard within a concentration of East Hollywood Thai restaurants that helped the community become officially recognized as the nation's first Thai Town in 1999, it moved to its Fairfax location near the Farmers Market and CBS Television sometime between 1974 and 1976.

WAT THAI TEMPLE, SUN VALLEY

WOMEN'S RIGHTS IN LOS ANGELES

The Women's Rights in Los Angeles Context, completed in 2018, focuses specifically on places associated with the struggle to improve the lives of women and children, from the suffrage movement beginning in the 1880s through the feminist movement of the 1970s. Its wide-ranging themes address: civic reform movements, from temperance to suffrage, during the Progressive Era; workplace emancipation of women during World War II; women's political organizations in a suburbanizing city after the war; and a reawakening of women's activism through Second Wave Feminism in the 1960s and 1970s.

Los Angeles and the Suffrage Movement

Numerous Los Angeles women and organizations played a significant role in the suffrage movement. The Friday Morning Club at 930–940 S. Figueroa St., founded by Caroline Severance in 1891, grew to become the largest women's club in California. It brought to Los Angeles nationally known activists such as Susan B. Anthony, Julia Ward Howe, and Charlotte Perkins Gilman, inspiring women to become engaged politically. Los Angeles women—including women of color, organized in groups such as the Sojourner Truth Industrial Club and the Helping Hand Society—played an unheralded role in the successful campaign to give women the right to vote.

The Anna Howard Shaw and Cora Scott Pope Residence (200 N. Avenue 66, Garvanza) is associated with two well-known national figures in the suffragist movement. Shaw was a physician, one of the first ordained female Methodist ministers in the U.S., a close associate of Susan B. Anthony, and held a leadership position in the National Woman Suffrage Association (NWSA). Shaw and Pope bought the land in 1886 while they were still living in Boston, but the home became a focal point for political organizing, serving as the site of an early Woman's Christian Temperance Union "Woman's home." Written accounts indicate that Shaw and Pope were forced to sell the house in 1897, after the failure of the 1896 California suffrage ballot initiative.

Feminist Art and Culture

The burgeoning feminist movement of the early 1970s made Los Angeles an important national center for feminist culture, in the visual arts as well as theater. Womanspace, located in a former laundromat in Venice, became the first space for the exhibition and performance of women's art on the West Coast in 1972. The launch of the Los Angeles Feminist Theater (LAFT) in 1970 helped lead the formation of other feminist theater troupes all over the city.

The Woman's Building (1727 N. Spring St., Chinatown/Lincoln Heights) has been called the first independent feminist cultural institution in the world, committed to providing an outlet for women artists to proclaim their place in art history. In 1973, artist Judy Chicago, art historian Arlene Raven, and graphic designer Sheila Levrant de Bretteville came together to create the Feminist Studio Workshop, which moved in 1975 to this 1914 Beaux Arts Standard Oil Company Sales Department Building that had been designed by architect Myron Hunt. From 1973 to 1991, this facility stood in contrast to most major American museums and arts programs, which routinely excluded female artists. FSW and other leading feminist and lesbian art organizations hosted numerous programs and activities, including a full-scale gallery program, hundreds of art exhibitions, film screenings, lectures by feminist artists, and an annual writing series featuring noted feminist authors.

MEMORY AND MEANING
IN A CHANGING LOS ANGELES

The historic context work for SurveyLA has laid important groundwork for the preservation of the places that shaped the development of each of these important communities. The documents highlighted here give both community members and decision-makers a sound basis to evaluate the significance of places associated with these often under-appreciated histories. But OHR has always seen this work as only a start—a jumping-off point for further activism, research, and governmental action to identify and protect these places.

It is important to note that most of the places identified in the contexts do not yet have formal historic designation. OHR has therefore partnered with several organizations, including Asian and Pacific Islander Americans in Historic Preservation (APIAHiP), to host a community-wide symposium aimed at spurring future nominations of sites for local and national historic designation. Also, while five of the largest Asian American groups were the focus of this initial work, the rich diversity within the Asian American and Pacific Islander (AAPI) communities, including Pacific Islanders, South Asians, and Southeast Asians, will offer future opportunities to engage with community leaders in telling both AAPI stories and the city's stories.

Historic preservation activities can be the basis for a Los Angeles where multiple layers of history are more visible, legible, and meaningful to all Angelenos.

THE WOMAN'S BUILDING, CHINATOWN-LINCOLN HEIGHTS

LIVE
COMEDY
HERE TONIGHT

LOS ANGELES

LOS ANGELES

DOWNTOWN'S
BROADWAY, WITH
THE LOS ANGELES
THEATRE, HCM #225

CHAPTER 5
SPARKING A DOWNTOWN RENAISSANCE:
L.A.'S ADAPTIVE REUSE PROGRAM

Great cities have a successful and vibrant downtown—a place that is the center of finance, government, retail, culture, and urban residential life. In the early decades of the twentieth century, Los Angeles had that type of downtown: in photos of Broadway or Spring Street during the 1920s and 1930s, there's an intense urban scene, with crowded sidewalks, abundant streetcars, bright neon lights, and a diverse cross-section of residents, shoppers, and entertainment patrons.

But as Los Angeles became a city of suburbs in the post-World War II era, new centers of activity developed throughout the region, the city morphed into a multi-centered metropolis, and Downtown lost its primacy as a "center of centers." By the 1990s, Broadway's twelve remarkable movie palaces were largely closed, as were

BROADWAY LOOKING NORTH FROM FIFTH STREET, CIRCA 1925

Downtown flagship department stores such as Bullocks, Robinson's, and May Company. The financial offices and banks of Spring Street, once known as the "Wall Street of the West," sat entirely vacant above the ground floor. Though still an active commercial office center, Downtown and its sidewalks were largely desolate after dark, when office workers went home. Throughout Downtown's historic core, open-air drug deals were more prevalent than pedestrians exploring the area to shop or dine.

But by 2010, Downtown Los Angeles looked very different. Thousands of Angelenos had moved into new housing in the area, spurring the opening of dozens of new restaurants, cafés, and retail stores and creating an accelerating demand for new high-rise housing towers.

While many factors have contributed to the revitalization of Los Angeles's Historic Downtown, the most important catalyst was arguably a single provision added to the City's Zoning Code: the Adaptive Reuse Ordinance (ARO).

Adaptive reuse refers to the conversion of an existing building to accommodate an activity different from its original purpose. There are many variants of adaptive reuse projects, such as train stations becoming retail centers or bank lobbies becoming restaurants. In Los Angeles, the most transformative adaptive reuse has involved the conversion of older commercial buildings into new housing units.

THE ABANDONMENT OF DOWNTOWN

The seeds for Downtown's more recent renaissance were laid decades ago through other urban policy choices—most notably the decision to largely abandon what was known for several decades as the "Historic Core" (later renamed "Historic Downtown"), an area roughly bounded by 2nd Street, Olympic Boulevard, Hill Street, and Main Street. Los Angeles instead created a sparkling new Downtown just to its west.

L.A.'s version of the urban renewal impulse that swept the nation during the 1950s and 1960s was spearheaded by the Los Angeles Community Redevelopment Agency (CRA), through the redevelopment of the Bunker Hill neighborhood. Bunker Hill had a rich architectural legacy. With the boom of the 1880s, the hill became the toniest neighborhood in the city, a prime locale for new mansions and luxury hotels. In 1901, the neighborhood was linked to the burgeoning commercial and financial district through the opening of the Angels Flight funicular—the "shortest railway in the world"—at the intersection of 3rd and Hill Streets.

As Los Angeles's residential development spread, many of Bunker Hill's mansions were subdivided into rooming houses. By the 1940s and 1950s, city officials viewed Bunker Hill as a "blighted" neighborhood—a perceived "slum" whose ills could only be cured through wholesale urban renewal, which in those days meant demolition and replacement. While other cities such as San Francisco rehabilitated its Victorian-era residential architecture, Los Angeles lost its largest and most intact neighborhood of Victorian homes and mansions.

In 1956, Los Angeles voters approved a ballot measure to eliminate a 150-foot height limit that had been in effect since 1904, which meant that no building at the time was taller than Los Angeles City Hall. In the 1960s and 1970s, a new financial district on Bunker Hill and to its south created a revived Downtown skyline with highrise office buildings, anchored by the Music Center on Grand Avenue.

All of these decisions and the resulting market trends left the previous Downtown core abandoned and largely vacant, yet still standing—freezing the district in a kind of urban benign neglect.

BUNKER HILL CLEARED FOR REDEVELOPMENT, 1971, WITH COMPLETED BUNKER HILL TOWER AND MUSIC CENTER

IRA YELLIN CREATED GRAND CENTRAL SQUARE APARTMENTS,
ABOVE GRAND CENTRAL MARKET AND
THE MILLION DOLLAR THEATRE.

EARLY ATTEMPTS TO REVIVE DOWNTOWN

Although the CRA's urban renewal policies had triggered this abandonment, by the 1980s and 1990s the agency had taken a leadership role in addressing these ills—and its primary tools became the adaptive reuse and rehabilitation of historic buildings. But these governmental investments soon proved to be ahead of their time.

The CRA's initial efforts focused on Spring Street, with an early adaptive reuse project involving two adjacent historic commercial buildings: rehabilitating the 1923 California Canadian Bank Building and the 1931 E.F. Hutton Building into a single condominium complex called Premiere Towers. CRA helped subsidize the conversion of the John Parkinson-designed Security Trust and Savings Building (1916) on Spring Street into a cutting-edge live-theater venue, the Los Angeles Theatre Center (LATC). However, both Premiere Towers and the LATC ended in financial insolvency for their owners and operators by the early 1990s.

In the early to mid-1990s, pioneering Downtown developer Ira Yellin, along with Levin and Associates Architects, pursued the conversion of Broadway's 1898 Homer Laughlin Building (where Grand Central Market has been the ground floor tenant for the past century), the 1905 Laughlin Annex, and the upper floors of the 1918 Million Dollar Theater Building into 121 apartment units. The CRA and Metropolitan Transportation Authority (MTA) invested heavily in the project, providing public subsidies that also allowed a portion of the units to be affordable. But just a few years later, the CRA and MTA needed to step up again with a financial bailout to help Yellin avoid foreclosure—underscoring that the initial bet on Broadway's historic rehabilitation was somewhat ahead of its time.

Many of the other former financial buildings along Spring Street and on nearby streets of the Historic Core became occupied by government agencies as low-rent satellite office spaces—or sat vacant altogether.

THE ADAPTIVE REUSE ORDINANCE

Amidst this backdrop of failed reinvestment in Downtown, Tom Gilmore, a newly minted developer who brought an urbanist's sensibility from New York, saw economic opportunity. In 1998, he purchased four massive buildings at Spring Street, Main Street, and 4th Street for $6.5 million, or only about $10 per square foot; the monumental Beaux-Arts-style Farmers and Merchants Bank Building sold for only about $100,000. The gregarious Gilmore articulated a vision of a twenty-four-hour Downtown, where younger, creative residents, empty nesters, and non-traditional households could find the lively and authentic urban environment

A PORTION OF TOM GILMORE'S OLD BANK DISTRICT PROJECT, INCLUDING THE 12-STORY BRALY BLOCK (CONTINENTAL BUILDING), DESIGNED BY JOHN PARKINSON IN 1904

that historic buildings can provide.

As Gilmore assembled funding and began advancing rehabilitation plans, he encountered challenges in the city's codes. The zoning code requirements were structured to guide new construction in more suburban settings, not the reuse of existing buildings. For example, new residential units were required to provide at least two on-site parking spaces per unit—space that simply wasn't available in a compact urban setting.

To address these issues, the City Planning Department developed a zoning ordinance, with advocacy leadership from Central City Association, and additional support from the Los Angeles Conservancy. The Adaptive Reuse Ordinance (ARO), approved by the city council in 1999, waived most zoning requirements for housing conversions: no new parking needed to be provided, and existing building conditions that did not conform to new zoning requirements could remain.

A companion effort addressed building code challenges, providing more flexible approaches to retrofitting these buildings for fire safety and structural stability. This was achieved first through guidelines and later, once the guidelines had been tested on actual projects, with permanent code amendments. Hamid Behdad, a former Department of Building and Safety official, led the city's Adaptive Reuse Program for three mayors, coordinating the response of city departments to help clear any remaining regulatory obstacles.

These relatively straightforward changes triggered some of the most striking results seen anywhere in the nation from a zoning code action. In just over a decade (1999 to 2010), the Adaptive Reuse Program facilitated the conversion of more than seventy older or historic structures in Downtown Los Angeles alone, creating more than 9,000 new housing units.

PRESERVATION PROFILE:
KARIN LILJEGREN

Karin Liljegren, FAIA, is the founding principal of Omgivning, a Los Angeles architecture and interior design firm. Before starting her firm, she spent sixteen years with Killefer Flammang Architects, where she was a project manager for many of the early Downtown adaptive reuse projects including the Old Bank District and the Pacific Electric Lofts. Her work has played an instrumental role in driving policies to encourage adaptive reuse projects.

I remember walking through the buildings that Tom Gilmore had purchased in 1999, when Downtown Los Angeles was not a place anyone went except for work. He was talking about his vision, and everybody on this walkthrough was just looking at each other as if to say, "He's crazy." The streets in the Historic Core at that time were literally empty—there were no homeless people or drug dealers: there was no humanity.

Tom knew that the Historic Core was destined to yet again become a vibrant neighborhood. Los Angeles had been lacking a true urban community, and was fortunate to have a large stock of rich historic buildings full of character and beauty. The idea was to renovate the buildings as inexpensively as possible (so the banks would lend to his crazy ideas), build simple,

big open spaces as loft apartments, and fill up the upper floors with residents. And then, he said, let's put art galleries in all of the ground floors—they're beautiful, they have lights on, so they're not empty storefronts. And then that was followed by calling it Gallery Row, and then a monthly art walk. At this point, it wasn't just Tom but other people as well. After there was a critical mass, then the retail and restaurants and bars followed, which fully activated a revitalized and new urban community.

None of this would have happened without the Adaptive Reuse Ordinance. You would have had to provide parking according to the current code, and you wouldn't have been able to do anything on the rooftop. Some of the upgrades inside the building were reduced slightly based on maintaining existing conditions, and we were able to do other things to make the building safer. It really helped keep the historic character of these buildings and allowed them to be upgraded significantly for fire/life safety.

I feel so fortunate to be able to walk into a building that's in a dilapidated state and be able to envision people in the spaces: how they can use it and adapt it for a new use. With these old buildings, the most important thing we can do is listen to what the building wants to be—not to come in with our own concept. No, there's already all this richness to its past

that we need to blend into the story of its future.

Places that have a sense of identity are the ones that are really going to thrive in the next ten, twenty, or fifty years. Retail is dying and globalization is creating a uniformity to a lot of architecture. With the new construction and high-rises that are being developed, it could be here, or in Vancouver or Atlanta—they all look the same. These historic structures in

Los Angeles create a sense of identity and place. We can densify our cities and still keep our historic buildings. So many people want to be in these old buildings. They just have something you can't build today—more of a human connection. ✶

METRO 417 (SUBWAY TERMINAL BUILDING)

The Subway Terminal Building at 4th and Hill Streets opened as a Downtown office building in 1925. Designed by architects Schultze and Weaver, the firm that had also designed the nearby Biltmore Hotel two years earlier, the building featured a similar H-shaped floor plan and Beaux-Arts design with Italian Renaissance ornamentation.

What made the Subway Terminal Building unique, however, was that it was designed to be the terminal for a new subway system for Los Angeles—seven decades before the opening of the region's Metro Rail system. Earlier in his career, architect Leonard Schultze had worked on the design of New York's Grand Central Terminal (1913). The basement of the Subway Terminal Building was built out as a full-fledged terminal, meant to accommodate five tracks and up to thirty train cars at one time.

The Hollywood-Glendale-Valley line was envisioned as the crowning achievement of the Pacific Electric railway system, with a new underground segment providing a time savings for Downtown commutes to and from communities such as Glendale and Burbank. But, ultimately, only a single one-mile segment—between Glendale and Beverly Boulevards and Hill and 5th Streets Downtown—involved an underground tunnel. Nevertheless, the building was a significant transit hub; during World War II, 65,000 daily commuters passed through the building.

The last trains went through the tunnel in 1955, after which the federal government purchased the building and operated it for many years with offices for federal agencies. The city ultimately filled in the tunnel from Flower Street to Figueroa Avenue in 1967; the building went through an initial renovation for private offices in the 1980s.

THE SUBWAY TERMINAL BUILDING'S TRACK LEVEL, CIRCA 1950

■ METRO 417 APARTMENTS, 417 S. HILL ST., ENTRANCE
■ THE SUBWAY TERMINAL BUILDING/METRO 417 LOBBY, WITH PINK MARBLE FLOORS AND COFFERED CEILING

But as the office market in Historic Downtown declined, the building was primed for a new use by the early 2000s, as the ARO took effect. Forest City Development purchased the building in 2003 and converted its nearly 500,000 square feet of office space into "Metro 417" (echoing its 417 S. Hill Street address), with 277 loft-style apartments. This adaptive reuse design reflected a collaboration between Thomas P. Cox Architects and the legacy Los Angeles firm AC Martin Architects.

The magnificent office lobby became an elegant residential entrance with brass doors, a coffered ceiling, stately columns, and marble floors. The significant interior modifications were consistent with historic preservation standards, which were required given the building's listing in the National Register of Historic Places and as Historic-Cultural Monument #177. The interiors had been previously altered many times for office modernizations. In addition to utilizing the ARO, Forest City took advantage of two other preservation incentives to make the rehabilitation possible: the Mills Act Historical Property Contract program, which provided a property tax reduction, and Federal Historic Rehabilitation Tax Credits, which allowed Forest City to recoup 20 percent ($12 million) of the $60 million spent on rehabilitation.

Many of the units, as well as the rooftop terrace serving as a common area for all building residents, have spectacular views of Downtown, including Pershing Square, Bunker Hill, and the Financial District.

METRO 417 RESIDENTIAL UNIT

PACIFIC ELECTRIC LOFTS (PACIFIC ELECTRIC BUILDING)

Like the Subway Terminal Building, the Pacific Electric Building's history reflects an early form of transit-oriented development. Henry Huntington constructed the building in 1905 at the corner of 6th and Main Streets as the offices for the Pacific Electric Railway—once the largest interurban railway system in the world—and as the hub for P.E.'s streetcar lines to Downtown. It was considered Los Angeles's first skyscraper; standing nine stories high, it was the largest office building in the city when it opened. Architect Thornton Fitzhugh designed the building with elements of Richardsonian Romanesque and Beaux-Arts styles, with yellow brick masonry and arched Romanesque windows.

The building's top floors were home to the Jonathan Club, an elite men's social club that included a ballroom with soaring arches and a gymnasium, billiard room, smoking room, tap room, library, and roof garden. The Jonathan Club relocated to a building on Figueroa in 1924, and the space was converted to offices.

Since 1908, the basement has been home to Cole's Pacific Electric Buffet, one of the oldest restaurants in the city, which claims to have invented the French dip sandwich (a claim also staked by Phillipe the Original, further north in Downtown). The building was declared Historic-Cultural Monument #104, first for Cole's P.E. Buffet in 1972, and then for the building itself in 1989 with an amendment to the designation. The building was listed in the National Register of Historic Places in 2009.

Throughout the 1990s, however, the building sat largely vacant. It was used mostly for location shooting, for films including *Forrest Gump* (1994) and *L.A. Confidential* (1997). ICO Investment Group embarked on its adaptive reuse in 2002, and by 2005 had completed a massive rehabilitation project to create 314 new rental housing units, making it the largest housing conversion project completed under the ARO.

Killefer Flammang Architects divided half a million square feet of the building's former office space into large units with exposed steel trusses. The rehabilitation was one of the first Downtown residential adaptive reuse projects to include a "rooftop amenity space," including a rooftop pool, garden, and gym. On the ninth floor, where the Jonathan Club's ballroom had been, the project team created three unique, two-level penthouse lofts with ornate cornices, original columns, ironwork, and arched windows. The eighth floor's former Jonathan Club rotunda was transformed into a library for residents, complete with stained glass and white marble. The lobby contains a number of artifacts from the building's Pacific Electric use, and "DANGER" warnings remain set into the sidewalk on Main Street, where streetcars once entered.

The Pacific Electric Lofts utilized Federal Historic Rehabilitation Tax Credits, which provide an income tax credit equivalent to 20 percent of a project's rehabilitation expenditures, underscoring the important role that historic preservation financial incentives have played in making adaptive reuse projects possible.

■ THE PACIFIC ELECTRIC BUILDING'S 8TH AND 9TH FLOOR ROTUNDA, SHOWN IN 1907, WHEN IT WAS HOME TO THE ELITE JONATHAN CLUB
■ THE ADAPTIVE REUSE FOR PE LOFTS CONVERTED THE ROTUNDA INTO A LIBRARY AND LOUNGE FOR RESIDENTS.

EASTERN COLUMBIA LOFTS (EASTERN COLUMBIA BUILDING)

The Eastern Columbia Building, located on Broadway and 9th Street at the south end of the Broadway Historic Theater and Commercial District listed in the National Register, is one of the most spectacular and iconic Art Deco landmarks in Los Angeles. It was designed by architect Claud Beelman and opened in 1930 as the headquarters of the Eastern Outfitting Company (a chain of twenty-nine home furnishing stores) and the Columbia Outfitting Company (an apparel company that was a spinoff of Eastern). Both companies were owned by a Jewish Polish immigrant, Adolph Sieroty, and the locally prominent Sieroty family would retain ownership of the Eastern Columbia until the 1980s.

The building was granted an exception to Los Angeles's 150-foot height limit, so the dramatic clock tower, with its neon "Eastern" sign, soared to 264 feet. It was the city's second-tallest building (after Los Angeles City Hall), dominating the south portion of the Downtown skyline for decades. Its design includes zig-zag details, geometric shapes, chevrons, a golden sunburst at the entrance, and distinctive turquoise terra cotta. The building is listed as HCM #294.

In later decades, the Sieroty family businesses closed, and the building became offices; by the 1990s, most of the space was taken by fashion-related businesses, but the building had lost its luster and prominence.

In 2003, the building was sold to Kor Group, which had recently completed another prominent adaptive reuse project: the conversion of the former Mobil Oil Company building at 6th and Flower into the 322-unit Pegasus Apartments. Killefer Flammang Architects, with Kelly Wearstler Interior Design, spearheaded an $80 million renovation of the Eastern Columbia, converting it into 147 residential units. The building's historic clock was repaired and became a dramatic backdrop for a rooftop pool, terrace, fireplace, and fitness center.

Unlike the Subway Terminal and Pacific Electric Building projects, which created rental units, the

EASTERN COLUMBIA BUILDING EXTERIOR, 2020

Eastern Columbia Lofts were marketed as for-sale condominiums. The building has become one of the premier homeownership options within Historic Downtown—actor Johnny Depp lived in a penthouse unit from 2007 to 2017—and has fostered a new close-knit community of homeowners. Like the Pacific Electric Lofts, the Eastern Columbia has benefited from historic preservation incentives: the City's Mills Act Historical Property Contract program provides owners with a property tax reduction, which allows the homeowners association to finance ongoing rehabilitation needs.

■ EASTERN COLUMBIA BUILDING CLOCK TOWER, VIEWED FROM THE BUILDING'S ROOFTOP TERRACE AND POOL, 849 S. BROADWAY
■ EASTERN COLUMBIA LOFTS LOBBY

BISCUIT COMPANY LOFTS (NATIONAL BISCUIT COMPANY BUILDING)

The National Biscuit Company Building, constructed in 1925 for what would later become Nabisco and situated in Downtown's growing industrial area, served the company's entire western region of eleven states. Considered one of the most advanced bakery plants in the world when it opened, it contained two separate plants—one producing a range of sweetened and unsweetened biscuits, and another dedicated to varieties of sugar wafers.

The building, designed by Eckel & Aldrich of St. Joseph, Missouri, is a seven-story, three-part structure with Art Deco and Classical Revival influences, with an exterior sheathed in brown mottled bricks and a granite base. Nabisco sold the property in the 1960s, and it served as a warehouse for many years. By the early 2000s, the 180,000-square-foot building was less than 40 percent occupied.

Linear City Development, a partnership of television producer Leonard Hill and developers Yuval Bar-Zemer and Paul Solomon, purchased the building in 2004 and completed an adaptive reuse project to produce 104 live/work lofts in 2006. Architect Aleks Istanbullu transformed the loading dock into a French bistro named Church & State, which created street vitality and an immediate sense of community within the building's industrial setting, establishing this portion of the Arts District as a restaurant destination. The design replaced storage sheds adjacent to the structure with a 12,000-square-foot garden and an in-ground saltwater swimming pool. The team also reconfigured the basement and added exterior decking to provide 154 on-site parking spaces.

All 104 live/work units sold out within one year. The "super-penthouse" space, converted from the old water tower, set a record for the highest price ever paid for a Downtown loft; it was owned at one point by actor Nicolas Cage. The live/work status of the building allowed for both residential life and economic activity: thirty small businesses were also located in the building.

The Biscuit Company Lofts broke new ground as the first major adaptive reuse project in the southern portion of the Arts District, demonstrating the strength of residential demand in an area previously defined by industrial uses.

THE SWIMMING POOL AND GARDEN, WHICH REPLACED THE FORMER BAKERY'S STORAGE SHEDS, PROVIDE VIEWS BACK TO THE NATIONAL BISCUIT COMPANY BUILDING.

■ BISCUIT COMPANY LOFTS RESIDENTIAL LOBBY
▨ NATIONAL BISCUIT COMPANY, HISTORIC EXTERIOR, CIRCA 1920S
▨ BISCUIT COMPANY LOFTS EXTERIOR, 1850 INDUSTRIAL ST., ARTS DISTRICT

BISCUIT COMPANY
LOFTS PENTHOUSE UNIT

WHY ADAPTIVE REUSE MATTERS: LEARNING FROM LOS ANGELES

Los Angeles's Adaptive Reuse Ordinance must be regarded as one of the most successful urban revitalization strategies of any city in recent decades—a straightforward set of governmental code changes that served as the catalyst for significant private sector investment.

But for all of its success, some critics have asserted that ARO has caused gentrification in Downtown, displacing lower-income residents. These critiques note the proximity of Los Angeles's Skid Row, or Central City East, with its high concentration of homeless services, just a few blocks east of Historic Downtown. However, the ARO did not result in the direct physical displacement of low-income residents; the vast majority of buildings converted were commercial buildings that were entirely vacant above the ground floor. The Los Angeles City Council also later passed an ordinance requiring one-for-one replacement of converted residential hotel or single-room-occupancy units, to further disincentivize the loss of units that typically rent to lower-income tenants.

A valid criticism of the ARO is that it failed to generate significant new affordable housing. Because Downtown land became increasingly pricey and government affordable housing funding was scarce during this period, only 797 units out of the more than 9,000 new units created between 1999 and 2010 were income-restricted based on federal regulations. As Downtown has become increasingly economically stratified—now largely a place for the wealthy or poor—subsequent plans have proposed new incentives for affordable housing.

Nevertheless, the ARO's role in transforming Downtown has benefited all of Los Angeles in numerous ways:

- It rescued dozens of architecturally distinctive and historically significant buildings from a likely fate of continued deterioration or potential demolition, not only preserving detail and craftsmanship that could not possibly be replicated today, but also fostering an important sense of history and place in the heart of the city.
- It created new housing supply in a city constantly struggling to keep up with its need for housing production.
- It added units in locations already well-served by existing infrastructure, including the heart of the city's growing Metro Rail system.
- It helped improve the region's air quality and minimize new traffic impacts by providing new units near major job centers, rather than in far-flung suburban or exurban locations accessible only through long freeway commutes.

Adaptive reuse also created a new residential base to support economic vitality in the heart of the city, sparking a rebound in Downtown nightlife not seen for many decades. While the 1999 opening of Downtown's Staples Center arena for Lakers and Clippers basketball and Kings hockey teams also helped establish a new nightlife anchor, the thousands of new residents now living in Downtown 365 days a year provided an economic base for retail stores, clubs, and restaurants. Downtown has become the epicenter of a culinary boom in Los Angeles.

While not every city has the high concentration of vacant historic buildings found in the Los Angeles of the 1990s, the ARO's basic formula—facilitating historic rehabilitation as an economic development tool—offers a replicable model for cities across the nation.

THE 1990S CONVERSION OF THE BULLOCKS WILSHIRE SPECIALTY STORE TO SOUTHWESTERN LAW SCHOOL SERVED AS AN EARLY MODEL FOR HOW L.A.'S HISTORIC BUILDINGS COULD ACCOMMODATE NEW USES.

CHAPTER 6
TRANSFORMING PLACES: CREATIVE REUSE AND REHABILITATION AROUND LOS ANGELES

The power of adaptive reuse and historic rehabilitation has not been limited to the Downtown Los Angeles renaissance. Historic rehabilitation has been taking hold all around Los Angeles, demonstrating the potential of historic buildings to fulfill broader community needs and create an enhanced sense of place in neighborhoods. It is so effective because it taps into several larger societal forces and values, including the human quest for authenticity, community, and continuity.

Authenticity

Historic places inherently convey an authenticity and character that cannot be replicated, since they are rooted in a rich past and use materials shaped by skill and craft. Increasingly, today's young adults say that they crave and seek out this type of authenticity. A 2017 survey by the National Trust for Historic Preservation found that more than half of millennials view historic preservation as important through the lens of engaging in authentic experiences. Millennials are twice as likely to prefer shopping or eating in historic downtowns (52 percent) and in places with historic appeal (49 percent) over malls and planned commercial districts (26 percent) or recently constructed places (22 percent).

Community

The historic buildings adapted for new purposes are mostly places that have long served as community anchors—visual landmarks in their neighborhoods or well-loved local institutions. Transforming these places and infusing them with new uses builds upon decades of local identification and connection, drawing immediately upon an accessible reservoir of goodwill. As Tom Mayes of the National Trust for Historic Preservation wrote in his 2018 book, *Why Old Places Matter*, "Old places foster community by giving people a sense of shared identity through landmarks, history, memory, and stories . . . Old places are where people, time, and place intertwine to form community."

Continuity

Mayes also argues in his book that, in a constantly changing world, old places give people a sense of orientation and connectedness to time that is essential to their psychological and emotional well-being. Architecture critic Paul Goldberger struck similar themes in a 2003 lecture, "On Preservation":

> . . . [Preservation] uses the past not to make us nostalgic, but to make us feel that we live in a better present, a present that has a broad reach and a great, sweeping arc, and that is not narrowly defined, but broadly defined by its connections to other era, and its ability to embrace them in a larger, cumulative whole. Successful preservation makes time a continuum, not a series of disjointed, disconnected eras.

In most major cities, the construction of new buildings as shiny new objects emerging from the ground tends to capture public attention and attract elected officials to celebratory ground-breaking ceremonies. Yet the Los Angeles experience demonstrates that it is actually the reuse and rehabilitation of older structures that can successfully address the most compelling challenges facing today's cities, including the housing crisis, economic vitality, and sustainability/climate change.

Housing

In cities like Los Angeles with a severe crisis in homelessness and affordable housing, adaptive reuse can provide the most direct path to creating new housing supply. Because a historic building is already constructed and well-accepted in its community, its conversion to housing can happen relatively quickly: reuse does not typically trigger community opposition or lengthy

THE FORMER SANTA FE COAST LINES HOSPITAL/LINDA VISTA HOSPITAL IN BOYLE HEIGHTS, BUILT IN 1905, WAS CONVERTED TO 97 UNITS OF SENIOR AFFORDABLE HOUSING IN 2015 AFTER REMAINING VACANT FOR TWO DECADES.

delays in the project approvals necessary to build new housing from the ground up.

Economic Efficiency and Economic Vitality

Rehabilitation frequently costs less than demolition and new construction, and it also makes long-term economic sense. This has been confirmed in several studies by the nation's largest landlord and developer, the U.S. General Services Administration (GSA), which provides workspace for more than a million federal employees. For example:

> . . . Cleaning, maintenance, and utility costs at GSA-controlled historic buildings have been

consistently lower than comparable operating costs for non-historic GSA buildings. . . . Contemporary interior finishes using man-made materials are more likely to require frequent renewal or replacement in contrast to generously dimensioned natural finish materials such as stone and wood, designed to last indefinitely with routine maintenance. (General Services Administration, *Held in Public Trust*, 1999)

Because rehabilitation often requires more skilled and local labor than new construction, rehabilitation activity recirculates more money in the local economy, creating more jobs and overall economic activity. A study of the economic impacts of preservation in California by Donovan Rypkema found that $1 million spent in new construction generates 26.5 jobs and adds $753,000 to local incomes, while the same $1 million used to rehabilitate a historic building creates 31.1 jobs and $833,000 added to local incomes.

Sustainability and Climate Change

Pursuing rehabilitation rather than demolition and replacement conserves natural resources. It reduces waste and construction materials in our landfills, as well as the need to harvest new building materials for new construction. Despite perceptions that historic buildings may have leaky windows or not be as energy efficient as new construction, the opposite is more frequently true: historic buildings usually already have design features that minimize the need for artificial heating and cooling, such as thicker walls, natural light, and cross-ventilation.

Rehabilitation and adaptive reuse have important roles to play in minimizing climate change, by reducing carbon emissions. As architect Carl Elefante succinctly stated, "The greenest building is the one that's already built." A 2011 study by the National Trust for Historic Preservation found that, even if a new building is 30 percent more energy efficient than a historic building, it would take between ten and eighty years to overcome the negative impacts on carbon emissions from the energy expended by demolition and new construction.

By tapping into our desire for authenticity, community, and continuity, rehabilitation and adaptive reuse are fulfilling important human needs in urban environments while also addressing such central challenges as housing, economic vitality, and climate change in communities around Los Angeles and across the nation.

BULLOCKS WILSHIRE/SOUTHWESTERN LAW SCHOOL, WILSHIRE CENTER/ KOREATOWN

While most of L.A.'s adaptive reuse projects have been twenty-first century conversions, it was a 1990s project that helped jumpstart the adaptive reuse trend: the conversion of the iconic Bullocks Wilshire specialty store into Southwestern Law School's administrative offices and law library.

When Bullocks Wilshire opened in 1929, its 241-foot tower soared above the 150-foot-high buildings that defined Downtown; its height was exceeded in Los Angeles only by City Hall. It was a pioneering art deco design by the father and son architectural team of John and Donald Parkinson. The magnificent store immediately at-

BULLOCKS WILSHIRE, NOW SOUTHWESTERN LAW SCHOOL, 3050 WILSHIRE BLVD., WILSHIRE CENTER

tracted affluent customers from nearby neighborhoods such as Hancock Park and Windsor Square, as well as Hollywood elite from Marlene Dietrich to Greta Garbo and Clark Gable. Generations of Angelenos fondly remembered shopping excursions to Bullocks Wilshire to purchase clothing for special occasions, often capped off by tea or lunch in the fifth-floor Tea Room.

Unlike traditional stores in urban downtowns, whose entrances were oriented to pedestrians on the street, Bullocks Wilshire was the first department store oriented to customers arriving by automobile. Its grand entrance was under a porte cochere and decorated with a ceiling mural by Herman Sachs called *The Spirit of Transportation*. Every room of Bullocks Wilshire featured a unique design aesthetic, and often artwork, that complemented the merchandise sold within its space.

By the late 1980s, however, the Bullocks stores had been sold to Macy's, which operated Bullocks Wilshire as an I. Magnin specialty store for its final years. Soon after the 1992 civil unrest damaged the store's ground floor, the store closed in 1993, and Macy's removed many of Bullocks Wilshire's iconic interior fixtures, dispersing them to other stores around the country. However, the Los Angeles Conservancy led a successful public campaign to convince Macy's to return the fixtures.

In 1994, the nearby Southwestern Law School purchased the Bullocks Wilshire building and worked with the architectural firm Altoon and Porter on its adaptive reuse. Southwestern meticulously restored historic features while creatively converting the various department spaces into a working law school. About a third of

■ BULLOCKS WILSHIRE FIRST FLOOR—THE FORMER PERFUME HALL/COSMETICS DEPARTMENT—
DESIGNED BY JOCK PETERS, WITH ST. GENEVIEVE MARBLE-COVERED WALLS
■ SOUTHWESTERN'S LEIGH H. TAYLOR LAW LIBRARY REFERENCE SECTION, WITHIN THE FORMER BULLOCKS WILSHIRE
SPORTSWEAR DEPARTMENT, FEATURING THE MURAL *THE SPIRIT OF SPORTS*, BY GJURA STOJANO

the building space is dedicated to the Leigh H. Taylor Law Library (named after the dean who spearheaded the adaptive reuse), which is the second-largest private academic law library in California. The remainder of the building features tiered classrooms and seminar spaces with multimedia technology, a practice courtroom, faculty and administrative offices with floor-to-ceiling windows, and garden terraces with panoramic views of the city. Even the legendary Tea Room has an appropriate new use as a dining room and cafeteria for students and faculty.

The Bullocks Wilshire adaptive reuse provides a compelling lesson on how historic buildings can be reimagined to serve the needs of today's students—a lesson that was unfortunately lost in 2005, when the L.A. Unified School District chose to demolish, rather than adapt for educational use, the historic Ambassador Hotel (1921), just a half mile west of Bullocks Wilshire on Wilshire Boulevard.

THE OAK-PANELED OFFICE OF THE DEAN OF SOUTHWESTERN LAW SCHOOL, ORIGINALLY AN APARTMENT AND OFFICE SUITE WHERE JOHN BULLOCK WOULD ENTERTAIN PROMINENT MEN WHILE THEIR WIVES WERE SHOPPING

28TH STREET APARTMENTS, SOUTH LOS ANGELES

Built in 1926 in the Spanish Colonial Revival style, the 28th Street YMCA was designed by Paul R. Williams, the first licensed African American architect west of the Mississippi. The structure was the culmination of a significant fundraising campaign within the city's African American community. For decades, the YMCA served the South Los Angeles African American community as the site of important political and social gatherings, with a gymnasium, a swimming pool, meeting spaces, and fifty-two small dormitory-style rooms. The property was designated as Historic-Cultural Monument #851 in 2006 and listed in the National Register of Historic Places in 2009.

Two non-profit developers, the Coalition for Responsible Community Development and Clifford Beers Housing, partnered in 2011 to rehabilitate the building as 28th Street Apartments, serving low-income residents, youths transitioning out of the foster care system, and special-needs adults. The second through the fourth floors of the existing building were rehabilitated to provide twenty-four studio units, complete with kitchenettes and bathrooms. The tile swimming pool was filled in with concrete to form the floor of the apartment's common room and kitchen; however, an outer edge of original tile defines the outline of the pool and, if the concrete is ever removed, the original tile would remain

ARCHITECT PAUL R. WILLIAMS, IN THE FRONT ROW, FIFTH FROM LEFT, POSES WITH MEMBERS OF THE 28TH STREET YMCA IN FRONT OF THE BUILDING.

28TH STREET YMCA, MAIN ENTRANCES, 1006 E. 28TH ST., SOUTHEAST LOS ANGELES

intact underneath.

A new five-story addition to the rear of the historic building provides twenty-five additional studio units. The addition was designed in a contemporary style by Koning Eizenberg Architecture (KEA), including a green roof, photovoltaic panels on the south elevation, and a perforated panel on the north side that gives way at the corners to frame views of the city.

The new addition's highly differentiated design was approved by the Office of Historic Resources and Cultural Heritage Commission, further demonstrating how designated properties can significantly evolve and accommodate a present-day architectural aesthetic.

■ JUXTAPOSITION OF KONING EIZENBERG ARCHITECTURE'S NEW RESIDENTIAL DESIGN WITH THE HISTORIC YMCA BUILDING
■ THE APARTMENTS' COMMON ROOM AND KITCHEN, CREATED BY FILLING IN THE FORMER SWIMMING POOL, WITH THE TILE EDGE REMAINING TO DEFINE THE POOL'S FORMER OUTLINE.

CDI EARLY LEARNING CENTER, CANOGA PARK

The Canoga Park Library in the West San Fernando Valley was part of a library bond campaign providing expanded library services to the burgeoning post-World War II suburban communities around Los Angeles. Designed in 1959 by architects Ralph Bowerman and Charles Hobson, Canoga Park's library had a virtual twin in Woodland Hills just a few miles away, designed by the same architects.

One of the first buildings to use thin-shell concrete construction, the Canoga Park Library has dramatic curved eaves and a parabolic roof. In the late 1990s and early 2000s, a new library bond financed the replacement of older libraries with larger facilities of nearly double the size, and library officials began to view the Mid-Century Modern West Valley libraries as obsolete.

In 2001, the Woodland Hills Library was demolished; however, the city's library department agreed not to oppose the designation of the Canoga Park Library as Historic-Cultural Monument #700. A new and larger Canoga Park Library was built about a mile away in 2004, leaving its former location vacant and dilapidated.

In 2007, the Child Development Institute (CDI), with financial support from the Community Redevelopment Agency of Los Angeles (CRA/LA), adapted the original Canoga Park Library into its new Early Learning Center (ELC). ELC provides a free drop-in learning and play space for young children, with discovery zones, play areas, reading circles, and puppet shows. It also offers

CANOGA PARK LIBRARY/CDI EARLY LEARNING CENTER, REAR EXTERIOR

CDI EARLY LEARNING CENTER INTERIOR

referrals to other community services, including health care and child care, within a neighborhood that has a significant concentration of lower-income residents.

Through adaptive reuse, a building with a legacy of providing community—a library, as a free learning space—is now a reinvented, accessible community center. The library's sleek lines and soaring roof now provide an inspirational backdrop for community gatherings, visually conveying a Mid-Century Modern sense of optimism, openness, and possibility.

CANOGA PARK LIBRARY/CDI EARLY LEARNING CENTER,
7260 OWENSMOUTH AVE., CANOGA PARK

BOYLE HOTEL, BOYLE HEIGHTS

In Boyle Heights, the Boyle Hotel at First Street and Boyle Avenue (also known as the Cummings Block) is one of the oldest commercial structures in the city, dating from 1889. It was designed by W.R. Norton for community leaders George Cummings and his wife Maria del Sacramento Lopez, the daughter of one of the area's most prominent landowners, Francisco Lopez.

The commercial block opened during the same year that a streetcar first connected Boyle Heights to Downtown Los Angeles, with the upper floors converted into a hotel in 1891. It quickly became a social and political center for the community, and by 1894 was named Hotel Mount Pleasant. Commanding the top of a hill overlooking Downtown Los Angeles, the building had a prominent corner turret, as well as patterned brickwork and cast-iron storefront columns. By 1918, the upper stories had been converted to nineteen apartments. The building became known as Boyle Hotel for most of the twentieth century. In more recent decades, mariachi musicians who sought work in the adjacent plaza rented rooms in the hotel, earning it the nickname "Mariachi Hotel."

With advocacy from a new Boyle Heights Historical Society, the building was designated Historic-Cultural Monument #891 in 2007. In 2006, the non-profit affordable housing organization East Los Angeles Community Corporation (ELACC) acquired the building; from 2010 to 2012, ELACC rehabilitated the structure to create fifty-one units of affordable housing—thirty in the historic building and twenty-one in a new addition—as well as three ground-floor commercial spaces and a Mariachi Cultural Center. Architect Richard Barron, a long-time president of the city's Cultural Heritage Commission, oversaw the new construction and rehabilitation, which included restoration of missing architectural features such as the distinctive cupola atop the corner turret.

As a city block of Los Angeles's original transit-oriented development spurred by an 1880s streetcar line, Boyle Hotel is again a transit-oriented development, now directly across from a Metro light-rail station. Like the 28th Street YMCA, the Boyle Hotel project demonstrates how historic buildings can provide an additional source of affordable housing while accommodating compatible new housing construction.

THE ADDITION, ACCOMMODATING 21 AFFORDABLE HOUSING UNITS, FEATURES A CONTEMPORARY DESIGN WITH FLOOR LEVELS ALIGNED WITH THE BOYLE HOTEL-CUMMINGS BLOCK.

First St. West from Hollenbeck.

GILMORE GAS STATION, HOLLYWOOD

Gilmore Gas Station was built in 1935 on land owned by actor Wallace Beery, at the corner of Highland and Willoughby Avenues in the south portion of Hollywood. Constructed in the Streamline Moderne style, it conveyed an image of cleanliness, movement, and efficiency.

At the time, Gilmore Oil Company was one of the largest oil producers; the Gilmore family also built and operated the Farmers Market and Gilmore Field, home of the Pacific Coast League's Hollywood Stars baseball team, in the nearby Fairfax district.

In later years, the gas station served as a popular backdrop for films and television commercials, including *48 Hours* (1982) and Steve Martin's *L.A. Story* (1991). Although it was designated as Historic-Cultural Monument #508 in 1992, the building sat vacant for twenty years and became increasingly dilapidated; in 2009, a truck accident severely damaged the building's canopies.

The precarious historic gas station found an unlikely rescuer a few years later: Starbucks Coffee. In 2015, Starbucks completed an adaptive reuse of the building, transforming the structure into a neighborhood coffee house. The existing openings in the gas station structure were turned into a drive-through window and a walk-up window, and a seating area was installed. Working closely with OHR staff and a preservation consultant, Starbucks kept existing features of the building intact and made the cantilevered canopies structurally sound; incompatible elements such as metal roll-up garage doors were replaced with contemporary adaptations of historic doors. Starbucks agreed to adapt its standard signage by using a smaller logo that was more fitting to the theme.

Through Starbucks's initiative, an auto-oriented landmark that had fueled local vehicles for decades is now fueling Angelenos in a new way, further demonstrating how historic buildings can be reimagined and repurposed to serve daily community needs.

GILMORE GAS STATION, 853-859 N. HIGHLAND AVE., HOLLYWOOD, HISTORIC (UNDATED)

■ GILMORE GAS STATION, BEFORE REHABILITATION
■ GILMORE GAS STATION, AFTER REHABILITATION

LINCOLN PLACE APARTMENTS, VENICE

Lincoln Place Apartments is a 1951 Mid-Century garden apartment complex designed by Heth Wharton and African American designer Ralph Vaughn, the team also responsible for Chase Knolls Apartments in Sherman Oaks. Like Chase Knolls, Lincoln Place embodied principles of the "Garden City" movement of urban planning and design: plentiful landscaping, curved pedestrian walkways, the promotion of social interaction through shared outdoor spaces, and the separation of pedestrians from the automobile through a "superblock" design.

What set Lincoln Place apart from Chase Knolls and other garden apartment complexes was, in part, its sheer size; Lincoln Place was originally constructed with 795 units, spread out in fifty-two buildings over thirty-eight acres.

But by the 1990s, the owner of Lincoln Place was eyeing the low-slung buildings and ample open space as an opportunity to build higher-density condominiums. The owner began evicting tenants, and those who remained formed a tenant association. In 2002, Amanda Seward, an attorney who helped gain historic district status for her own Mid-Century Modern neighborhood, submitted a nomination of Lincoln Place to the National Register of Historic Places, kicking off a multi-year historic preservation battle. The debate was certainly about historic preservation, but a portion of the fight was also about the spirit of Venice—whether middle-class, more modestly priced housing could endure in a rapidly changing community.

In early 2003, while final action on the National Register nomination was still pending, the property was purchased by a new owner—Aimco, which secured demolition permits for two buildings. While the tenant association and a coalition of preservation groups appealed and filed lawsuits to block demolition in mid-2003, five additional buildings were demolished, for a total of ninety-nine units. Aimco followed up from 2004 to 2006 by relocating the remaining tenants, amidst continued litigation and countersuits. In 2005, having failed to secure final approval of National Register status, Seward and the Lincoln Place tenants took their preservation advocacy to the state, where the State Historical Resources Commission voted to determine Lincoln Place as eligible for listing in the California Register. Nevertheless, when the sheriff's department arrived in December 2005 to evict the fifty-two remaining tenant households by force, it was said to be the largest Sheriff's Department lockout in Los Angeles history.

After the property had sat vacant for several years while legal challenges continued, the economic downturn of 2008 led to a change in direction: Aimco decided to rehabilitate the complex instead of demolishing it. Patti Shwayder of Aimco later explained the decision to *Preservation* magazine in 2016:

> It was clear the Venice community had a very special place in their hearts for Lincoln Place. And I think it's fair to say we didn't always appreciate the historic nature of the property.... We took a second, third, and fourth look to see what we could do with the existing property. And when we did that, we found retro buildings that we could turn retro-chic. We found natural hardwood floors that could be refinished and were really quite spectacular. We found each building had amazing windows and cross-ventilation and low-density features that were attractive.... So we began working on how we could move into an existing historic fabric with all these character-defining features and add modern conveniences that would make this a showpiece.

In all, forty-five buildings were rehabilitated and thirteen new buildings constructed to replace previously demolished structures, resulting in a blend of old and new. Through a settlement agreement reached in 2010, eighty-three evicted tenants were permitted to return at their previous rental rates, and 696 rehabilitated units were retained under the city's rent control law (Rent Stabilization Ordinance), maintaining some affordability in rental rates for longer-term residents.

In 2014, Lincoln Place had its grand reopening, and in 2015 the complex was listed in the National Register of Historic Places—this time, with Aimco's full support.

■ LINCOLN PLACE TWO-STORY RESIDENTIAL GROUPINGS, SET WITHIN AMPLE LANDSCAPING AND MATURE TREES
■ LINCOLN PLACE, WITH GEOMETRIC PATTERNS OF WOOD AND GLASS AT ENTRYWAY

PRESERVATION PROFILE:
LINDA DISHMAN

Linda Dishman, the president and CEO of the Los Angeles Conservancy, has led L.A.'s primary citywide and countywide non-profit historic preservation organization since 1992. The Conservancy has the largest membership of any local historic preservation organization in the country.

Since the Conservancy was founded in 1978 to save the Central Library, we've had two missions—education and advocacy. These were inextricably linked, because you can't successfully advocate if people don't understand why our historic buildings should be preserved.

The Conservancy started a film series, *Last Remaining Seats*, in 1987 because people hadn't been in the historic theaters on Broadway for decades. The idea was, if you don't know what's inside these buildings, you don't know why they should be saved. So one of the great joys of *Last Remaining Seats* is to stand by the entrance and watch people as they come in. You really can tell who has never been there, because their jaws drop, and they turn to their friends and say, "Look at this!" When they walk in, they know they're someplace special, and they leave as advocates for preservation.

We do a lot of work with kids. We've worked for over ten years with Heart of L.A. (HOLA), an after-school program for kids near MacArthur Park. Every year these kids explore their neighborhoods—the buildings they walk by every day, like Bullocks Wilshire or the American Cement Company building—and learn about why buildings look the way they look. Over the course of six sessions, their attitudes about their neighborhoods change, and they start talking with their families about what they've learned. That's why what we do is so meaningful; it's about changing people's perceptions of their neighborhoods and their city.

From the founding of the Conservancy, we've always been focused on the "win-win" solution. When the Century Plaza Hotel was threatened with demolition, there was a city council race. We made preservation of the hotel a campaign issue, and interviewed the top five candidates to figure out where they stood. Paul Koretz was ultimately elected as the councilmember, and within his first two weeks in office he announced that he would initiate historic designation of the hotel. Just that statement was enough to bring the developer to the table to work with us and figure out how to get the density he needed while still preserving the Century Plaza Hotel.

When the City of Los Angeles took on SurveyLA, it changed the whole dynamic of preservation. Though the Getty funded half of SurveyLA, the city still had to fund its half, which was the most significant investment we'd seen in preservation. SurveyLA also identified how much of the city is historic—at most 7 percent—so there is plenty of room for new density and development in the other 93 percent. We're often criticized as being anti-development, which is not true—and now we can say with certainty that there are lots of opportunities for new development within the city. Since we now know that such a small percentage is historic, all of us—including city government—need to work hard and make sure there's a policy commitment to keep those buildings, so they continue to tell the stories that make Los Angeles the city we all know and love. ✖

PRESERVATION PROFILE: BRENDA LEVIN, FAIA

Brenda Levin, FAIA, is the founding principal of Levin & Associates, a pioneering architecture firm in Los Angeles. The firm has led the preservation and renovation of significant Los Angeles cultural and civic landmarks, including Los Angeles City Hall, Griffith Observatory, the Oviatt Building, the Fine Arts Building, the Bradbury Building, the Wiltern Theatre/Pellissier Building, and Wilshire Boulevard Temple.

I arrived in Los Angeles from the East Coast in 1976, having just graduated from the Harvard Graduate School of Design. I was a reluctant transplant; my husband, David Abel, had just accepted a job here at the Coro Foundation, and I thought we would soon go back east. Both my graduate school colleagues and I had a bias that Los Angeles was the architectural wasteland of America.

Coro was moving its offices to the Oviatt Building, which had just been purchased by a developer named Wayne Ratkovich. I was put on the Oviatt project in part because of the perception that my East Coast background gave me some understanding of historic buildings. From 1978 to 1980, we were pretty much the only developer/architect team in Los Angeles looking at a historic building to anticipate what it could become—seeing beyond what it is, to what it could be.

In 1980, I left Group Arcon to create Levin & Associates, and continued to collaborate with Wayne on the Wiltern Theatre and Chapman Markets. Wayne was a pivotal figure in the Los Angeles preservation movement, and he graciously let me link my reputation to his wagon.

Ira Yellin was another developer who was smart, articulate, and had a strong sense of design. He had a vision for Grand Central Market, of how it could both retain its rich history while becoming a place for the new young Downtown residents to shop and eat, and also took on the renovation of the Bradbury Building. As with all historic buildings, there is the challenge

of incorporating new infrastructure without damaging the character, materials, and essence of a space, and how to deal with the building codes, which are written for new construction. When I brought the plans for the Bradbury Building to the fire department, they gave us corrections to enclose the stairs. I remember just being gobsmacked—my reaction was, "Have you ever been in the building?" We've now come a long way in allowing for alternatives that meet performance criteria of the code rather than the prescriptive code.

For L.A. City Hall, our work was to preserve the character of the building, but also to make it more accessible. Griffith Observatory remains my favorite public project because of the building, the site, and its visibility. It is rare to find someone who cannot tell you a story of their visit—as a child, parent, or grandparent. It touches everyone, welcomes everyone, and encourages everyone from young kids to seniors to think about our planet and what's beyond—where we fit in and how we connect.

During the early years, Levin & Associates was the known design firm working on historic building projects; I believe many architects did not find them as interesting or important as new construction. That's changed remarkably, and now there are many firms and developers who see the value of preservation. ✖

WILSHIRE BOULEVARD TEMPLE, WITH THE REM KOOLHAAS/OMA-DESIGNED EVENT CENTER UNDER CONSTRUCTION, 3663 WILSHIRE BLVD., WILSHIRE CENTER

WILSHIRE BOULEVARD TEMPLE, WILSHIRE CENTER/KOREATOWN

Wilshire Boulevard Temple is one of the most grandiose religious structures in Los Angeles, opened in 1929 and designed by A.M. Edelman with the architectural firm of Allison and Allison.

The temple was a testament to the vision and the leadership of Rabbi Edgar F. Magnin, known as "Rabbi to the Stars," who served as Wilshire Boulevard Temple's senior rabbi for a remarkable sixty-nine years (1915–1984). Magnin joined the westward movement of Angelenos during the 1920s, relocating Congregation B'nai B'rith, which had established Los Angeles's first synagogue in Los Angeles, from Downtown to an expanding Wilshire Boulevard. He enlisted Hollywood tycoons—including Sid Grauman, Louis B. Mayer, Carl Laemmle, and Irving Thalberg—to make donations supporting the temple's construction. The temple featured ornate marble, stained glass windows, and a soaring coffered dome, rising 110 feet above the sanctuary floor. The donations of studio executive Jack Warner and his brothers Harry and Abraham funded the creation of large murals in the sanctuary, painted by artist Hugo Ballin and depicting 3,000 years of Jewish history.

Wilshire Boulevard Temple was the largest and most prominent Jewish congregation in the city for decades. But by the 1990s, much of the congregation had moved further west, and the temple invested in creating a new campus on the Westside while still maintaining its historic building. The 1992 civil unrest led to the burning of numerous buildings on the surrounding blocks, in a neighborhood that increasingly became identified as Koreatown. Deferred maintenance put the building in jeopardy; at one point, a large chunk of plaster fell from the dome into the sanctuary, necessitating protective netting over the heads of congregants.

With the congregation facing a difficult choice of whether to abandon its historic campus altogether, Senior Rabbi Steven Z. Leder instead articulated a vision for a rehabilitated temple and a recommitment to the temple's urban neighborhood. Longtime temple member and architect Brenda Levin, FAIA, spearheaded the rehabilitation plan and also created a master plan for the campus's expansion that would include school buildings, a food pantry, and social services for the surrounding community. Like Rabbi Magnin before him, Rabbi Leder proved to be a masterful fundraiser, raising the $150 million necessary for the meticulous rehabilitation and compatible new construction.

While accepting a Los Angeles Conservancy Preservation Award for the rehabilitation, Rabbi Leder eloquently explained the power of the project:

> Our ancestors gave us the magnificent Wilshire Boulevard Temple. We undertook the massive effort to bring it back to its original luster and beauty under the brilliant hand of Brenda Levin, who is surely one of Los Angeles's great treasures. We did this because we want to be good ancestors. We did this because we believe in the heart of Los Angeles, physically and spiritually. We did this because the core of every great city regenerates. We did this because we are the only Jewish institution in the most ethnically diverse council district in America west of Brooklyn, and we believe in loving our neighbors as we love ourselves . . .. We did this because we believe in the power and the inspiration of great architecture—which is, after all, its own form of spirituality and prayer.

The revitalized temple not only provides a tangible connection to the glorious past of this congregation, but is also a touchstone for inter-group collaboration in a neighborhood that is today primarily Korean American and Latino. The final phase of the campus, under construction for a planned late-2020 opening, is a dramatic new event center designed by internationally known architects Rem Koolhaas/OMA. The city's Cultural Heritage Commission found the new building to be an appropriate addition to this Historic-Cultural Monument property. The OMA design illustrates how a dramatically contemporary building can coexist with a historic religious structure, using a distinct architectural vocabulary yet bending away from the temple in deference to the historic structure.

■ THE TEMPLE'S RESTORED STAINED GLASS ROSE WINDOW DEPICTS A TORAH SCROLL AND STAR OF DAVID IN THE CENTER AND SYMBOLS OF THE TWELVE TRIBES OF ISRAEL IN ITS OUTER CIRCLE.
▪ WILSHIRE BOULEVARD TEMPLE: VIEW OF THE SANCTUARY WITH ITS RESTORED AND STABILIZED BYZANTINE REVIVAL-STYLE COFFERED DOME CEILING.

CBS COLUMBIA SQUARE STUDIOS, HOLLYWOOD

In 1937, when CBS head William S. Paley wanted a West Coast headquarters, he hired noted architect William Lescaze, who had designed the PSFS Building in Philadelphia, the first International Style skyscraper in the U.S. Lescaze created a progressive new studio complex in the heart of Hollywood: CBS Columbia Square (1938), designed in the International Style with some Streamline Moderne features (such as porthole windows).

Many of the classic CBS Radio broadcasts originated from Columbia Square, most frequently from legendary "Studio A," including the *The Jack Benny Program*, *The Burns and Allen Show*, *The Bing Crosby Show*, *The Red Skelton Show*, and *Gunsmoke*. In 1951, Lucille Ball and Desi Arnaz filmed the pilot for *I Love Lucy* at Columbia Square, before the studio's television production moved the following year to a dedicated new facility, CBS Television City in the Beverly-Fairfax district. Columbia Square then became a center for recording music by popular artists such as Frank Sinatra, the Beach Boys, the Byrds, Janis Joplin, and Led Zeppelin, as well as the Columbia Symphony Orchestra conducted by Bruno Walter.

But by 2007, the remaining CBS Radio operations had moved to other facilities, and Columbia Square was sitting vacant with its future in doubt. Two years later, the preservation organization Hollywood Heritage successfully nominated Columbia Square for Historic-Cultural Monument status, paving the way for adaptive reuse of Columbia Square that would also allow for significant new development on vacant surrounding portions of the property.

NeueHouse, a New York-based private workspace collaborative serving a "culturally nomadic membership," made Columbia Square its first West Coast out-

■ CBS COLUMBIA SQUARE STUDIOS, CIRCA 1948
■ INTERIOR VIEW OF COLUMBIA SQUARE'S RADIO BUILDING, GROUND FLOOR AND SECOND LEVEL, REUSED AS NEUEHOUSE, WITH OPEN WORKSPACES SURROUNDED BY CONFERENCE ROOMS.

VIEW OF COLUMBIA SQUARE, 6121 SUNSET BLVD., HOLLYWOOD, WITH KILROY DEVELOPMENT'S BUILD-OUT OF THE CAMPUS: INCLUDING OFFICES FOR VIACOM AND A TWENTY-STORY RESIDENTIAL TOWER.

post, leasing all six stories of the CBS Radio building as well as a three-story office building on the property. The interiors were transformed by New York architect David Rockwell, who also designed the interior of Hollywood's Dolby Theatre. Members of NeueHouse have access to all of Columbia Square's facilities, including post-production and broadcast spaces, a screening room, and a private dining room. Studio A became a two-story theater for events, and the former recording studios have become conference rooms.

Kilroy Development added a twenty-story, 200-unit residential tower to the property: Columbia Square Living, which includes a mix of high-end apartment units, including units for corporate housing and extended stay. In 2017, the entertainment giant Viacom—which includes MTV, Comedy Central, and BET—moved its West Coast headquarters from Santa Monica to a new six-story building at Columbia Square. The new headquarters, topped by a large blue "Viacom" sign, has brought more than 850 additional employees into Hollywood.

Through the Columbia Square project, a historic space associated with traditional broadcast media has been reimagined to incubate the diverse creative media of the twenty-first century, while also accommodating new housing.

ARCHITECT WILLIAM LESCAZE SOFTENED COLUMBIA SQUARE'S INTERNATIONAL STYLE ARCHITECTURE BY INCORPORATING STREAMLINE MODERNE DESIGN ELEMENTS, SUCH AS NAUTICAL-THEMED PORTHOLE WINDOWS AND STAIR RAILINGS, CURVED WALL FEATURES, AND ELEVATOR FLOOR INDICATOR.

SPRUCE GOOSE HANGAR, PLAYA VISTA

In 1943, Howard Hughes built a 319,000-square-foot building to house the construction of an H-4 Hercules flying boat known as the *Spruce Goose*, designed by Hughes's company during World War II. The *Spruce Goose* cost $23 million to construct (about $300 million in 2020), was built entirely of wood, and was the first aircraft with a wingspan longer than a football field. Yet it flew only once, for 26 seconds and about one mile, in 1947. For decades, its massive hangar sat vacant and was used as a soundstage for films such as *Titanic* (1997) and *Avatar* (2009). The *Spruce Goose* itself has long been a subject of public fascination: it remained on display along the waterfront in Long Beach, near the *Queen Mary* ocean liner, from the 1970s through the early 1990s. In 1992, the unique aircraft was moved to an aviation museum in Oregon.

Pioneering preservation developer Wayne Ratkovich, who had collaborated with architect Brenda Levin on the rehabilitation of Downtown's Oviatt Building and Fine Arts Building and Wilshire Center's Wiltern Theatre and Chapman Market in the 1970s and 1980s, again saw preservation opportunity in the *Spruce Goose* hangar and ten other abandoned buildings from Howard Hughes's heyday. Ratkovich acquired the entire property in 2010 for $32 million and rebranded the complex around its *Spruce Goose* identity, changing its name from Hughes Industrial to the Hercules Campus.

Levin developed adaptive reuse plans of the historic industrial buildings for creative office space, and EPT Design created a landscape plan that emphasized flexible open spaces meant to entice creative employees. The Hercules Campus attracted a YouTube production studio in 2012. Historic buildings and authenticity create economic value; as Ratkovich told the *Los Angeles*

HOWARD HUGHES'S *SPRUCE GOOSE* (H-4 HERCULES) ON ITS ONLY FLIGHT, 1947

Times in 2012, "It is just amazing how companies prefer these industrial buildings to squeaky-clean, brand-new structures."

The historic campus has become the hub of "Silicon Beach"—Yahoo, Facebook, and Microsoft all have a presence nearby in Playa Vista. The *Spruce Goose* hangar itself, given its sheer size, was one of the last pieces of the Hercules Campus to fall into place. When Google leased the hangar in 2015, ZGF Architects created a spectacular "building within a building," inserting a new interior four-story space with elevated walkways, connecting offices, common meeting areas, a fitness center, cafés, and event spaces.

Ratkovich sold the hangar in 2016 to the Japanese conglomerate ASO Group for $273 million—more than eight times what he had paid for the entire Hughes property just six years before.

The Hercules Campus and the *Spruce Goose* hangar offer an instructive case study on how creative, unconventional spaces created by an iconoclast can be adapted into the centerpiece of a city's creative cluster: Los Angeles's Silicon Beach.

■ *SPRUCE GOOSE* HANGAR, 16 S. CAMPUS CENTER DR., PLAYA VISTA, AS CREATIVE OFFICES FOR GOOGLE
■ ZGF ARCHITECTURE EXPOSED LONG-COVERED WINDOWS, FLOODING THE INTERIOR WITH LIGHT,
AND RESTORED THE HANGAR'S TIMBER BEAMS.
■ INTERIOR OF *SPRUCE GOOSE* HANGAR, WITH INTERIOR CIRCULATION
AND DINING/CAFE SPACES INSERTED WITHIN A PRESERVED CENTRAL SPINE

TRANSFORMING PLACES

CHAPTER 7
LOOKING AHEAD:
THE FUTURE OF HISTORIC PRESERVATION

For decades, Los Angeles and all of California have tended to face challenges ahead of the rest of the nation, whether tackling air quality and environmental issues as early as the 1970s, or grappling with contentious debates around immigration in the 1990s. The same holds true in historic preservation, where the city's innovations are leading the way for other regions.

But what is the next set of challenges that preservation will face in an ever-evolving Los Angeles? And how will these challenges—and the public response to these issues—yield lessons for the rest of the nation?

THE AFFORDABLE HOUSING CRISIS

Los Angeles, and California more generally, have been confronting an acute housing crisis. As of 2020, 92 percent of the homes sold in Los Angeles were considered unaffordable to those earning the region's median household income. Los Angeles County now has nearly 60,000 homeless residents, and homeless encampments in Los Angeles are no longer limited to particular areas of Downtown, but are found throughout the city.

California's housing crisis has, in turn, brought the rise of a new type of advocate: "YIMBYs" (Yes in My Backyard) who sought to counter the longtime power of homeowners groups and other organizations who took a NIMBY (Not in My Backyard) position opposing new housing development. YIMBYs have argued that only by creating more housing supply—housing of all kinds, in all locations—can we address the disconnect between housing supply and demand and bring prices down.

Many YIMBY advocates have gone further, arguing that historic preservation itself is one of the root causes of the housing crisis. Preservation protections are freezing entire neighborhoods in time, they argue, preventing change and more intense housing development that could address the crisis. Many also assert that single-family residential development represents a legacy of racial exclusion through a history of restrictive covenants, as well as "redlining" practices in lending, all of which combine to perpetuate inequities in who has opportunities to live in single-family homes.

These arguments have led to proposals for state legislation to override local zoning and land-use plans to allow larger-scale development near transit stops and to require municipalities to allow multiple units on all single-family zoned lots. Already, as of 2020, California's state laws on Accessory Dwelling Units (ADUs), or "granny flats," now allow a detached ADU as well as an additional "Junior ADU" attached to an existing single-family home, essentially permitting up to three units on any single-family property in the state.

Historic preservation advocates need to develop a sharper case for how "one-size fits all" state mandates can undermine the significant benefits of preservation. The significant economic and community benefits of historic districts will clearly dissipate if these neighborhoods no longer retain their distinctiveness.

Historic preservation and density are not mutually exclusive. The Preservation Positive Los Angeles study found that the number of residents per mile in Los Angeles's Historic Preservation Overlay Zones (HPOZs), or local historic districts, is actually 50 percent higher than the average residential density in the rest of the city. Residential density in L.A's HPOZs also exceeds the citywide persons per square mile in Boston, Chicago, and Washington, DC. Additionally, as Los Angeles's Adaptive Reuse Ordinance has shown, historic preservation can play a significant role in creating new housing supply. And preservation protections also help maintain those multi-family units that have more affordable rents since, in cities such as Los Angeles, only older units are covered by rent stabilization laws.

At the same time, preservation advocates should not automatically reject all policies driven by today's new housing reality. Los Angeles's early experience with ADUs, for example, indicates that new units added to the rear of a property need not undermine the overall character of a historic district. The updates of Community Plans in Los Angeles—in neighborhoods such as West Adams and South Los Angeles—also show zoning changes can accommodate increased housing opportunities in some areas, while also protecting historic resources and cohesive historic character in other neighborhoods identified through SurveyLA.

LIVABLE DENSITY AND ECLECTIC HOUSING OPTIONS WITHIN A HISTORIC DISTRICT: THE 2400 BLOCK OF SICHEL ST. IN THE LINCOLN HEIGHTS HPOZ INCLUDES A HIPPED ROOF COTTAGE, A SPANISH COLONIAL REVIVAL TRIPLEX, AND A PRAIRIE/CRAFTSMAN STYLE APARTMENT BUILDING.

PRESERVING THE RECENT PAST

As time marches on, newer buildings and places continually emerge as suitable objects of historic preservation. The National Register of Historic Places has a "Fifty-Year Rule" when it comes to considering nominations: buildings or places younger than fifty years old can still be listed in the register, but they must clear a higher bar in demonstrating "exceptional importance."

Yet, it is the architecture younger than fifty years old that is often most vulnerable to demolition. Cycles of taste in architectural styles mean that a particular design aesthetic typically reaches its nadir in public esteem much earlier than fifty years later—a low point that

Michael Kubo of the University of Houston has dubbed "Ugly Valley."

As an example, the art deco architecture of the late 1920s and 1930s was considered obsolete in many cities during the 1960s and 1970s, as seen in Los Angeles by the 1969 demolition of the Atlantic Richfield Tower (1929) and the late 1970s demolition threat to the Wiltern Theatre/Pellissier Building (1931). In the 1980s, threats to 1950s "Googie" coffee shops and Modern residences led Los Angeles Conservancy volunteers to create a group that evolved into the Conservancy's Modern Committee. This laid the groundwork for advocacy and awareness-building around Mid-Century Modernism that ultimately gave buildings from this period a unique cachet.

In the early 2020s, looking back even fifty years takes us into the architecture of the 1970s—a design era that conjures visions of shag carpets, wood-paneled interiors, and expansive atriums. Journeying back twenty-five to forty years into the depths of today's Ugly Valley brings us into the 1980s and 1990s, an architectural era often defined by Postmodernism with its Neoclassical motifs and bright pastel colors. But however they may appear to us today, these buildings are the next frontier for preservation advocacy.

When the field surveys for SurveyLA began in 2010, evaluating the historic significance of buildings built as late as 1980 already transcended the Fifty-Year Rule and went well beyond the practices of most other cities. But more than a decade later, one of the challenges for Los Angeles and other communities will be how to extend historic resource evaluations and designations into the more recent past, while remaining mindful of the often-blinding glare found within Ugly Valley.

CLIMATE HERITAGE

With the changing climate becoming the most urgent challenge facing our planet, "climate heritage," the intersection of climate change and cultural heritage, needs to be front and center for the historic preservation community.

For decades, historic preservation professionals and community activists have seen real estate development pressure as the main threat to significant historic resources—with the bulldozer looming large as the fearsome symbol of destruction. But with the accelerating impact of a changing climate, a very different set of threats is emerging, as changes in temperatures, rainfall, wind, soil conditions, and sea level are increasingly affecting our cultural resources.

We are already beginning to see these impacts in Southern California: widespread wildfires in 2019 destroyed many significant historic resources in the Santa Monica Mountains just outside L.A., such as the 1927 Peter Strauss Ranch and the Paramount Ranch Western Town, a popular Hollywood filming location. The unique heritage in Los Angeles's hillside neighborhoods is at greater risk due to fires sparked during more frequent extreme weather conditions. And many of the historic resources within L.A.'s lower-lying coastal communities, such as Venice, Playa del Rey, and portions of San Pedro and Wilmington, are at risk of inundation from sea level rise in the coming decades.

But even as climate change is increasingly imperiling historic resources, our historic resources also have an important role to play in minimizing the impacts of climate change. Preserving existing buildings is one of the most effective strategies to reduce carbon emissions. According to the Advisory Council on Historic Preservation, constructing a replacement for a 50,000-square-foot building releases the same amount of carbon into the atmosphere as driving a car 2.8 million miles.

But while preservation is always more carbon-efficient than demolition and replacement, the preservation community still needs to prioritize improving the energy efficiency of historic buildings even while preserving significant historic features. Since existing buildings are responsible for approximately 40 percent of carbon emissions, how do we find a climate heritage "sweet spot"—bringing existing buildings as close as possible to "net zero" carbon emissions while also maximizing the benefits of heritage conservation?

Historic preservation can also play a central role in helping our cities adapt to a changing climate. How do we begin to assess which cultural resources are at greatest risk from wildfire or sea level rise? In Los Angeles, can we use the data from SurveyLA to understand where our cultural heritage may be at greatest risk? And how can the qualities found in successful historic neighborhoods—strong cultural traditions, higher social cohesion, and walkability—help create more resilient communities in this era of rapid climate change?

The City of Los Angeles, through its OHR, is now participating in the Climate Heritage Network, a mutual support network of city, state/provincial, tribal, and historic preservation offices, together with non-governmental organizations (NGOs) and universities, all committed to helping their communities tackle climate change. In all major cities, historic preservation leaders will need to collaborate with environmental leaders and sustainability experts, preparing themselves for the cultural heritage impacts of a changing climate and reducing their own carbon emissions from older buildings to help meet the global climate challenge.

ELEVATING PRESERVATION WITHIN ALL COMMUNITIES

The early decades of historic preservation activism across America focused heavily on places whose histories primarily reflected the contributions of white/Anglo males. But Los Angeles is now one of the most diverse cities in the world. U.S. Census Bureau estimates from 2017 placed the percentage of non-Hispanic/Latino white population in L.A. at 28 percent and falling.

These demographic realities make it even more urgent for historic preservation to prioritize the stories and needs of all communities within the city. Many of these communities have a more recent history in L.A., with places that are only beginning to be appreciated for their historic significance. For example, the Salvadoran and Guatemalan communities only began forming in Los Angeles during the 1980s; this period also saw the most significant growth of the Korean community. Although it may take some additional time or perspective for the places associated with these formative L.A. histories to come of age, historic preservation initiatives can help accelerate these efforts and interpret these experiences.

The work of the OHR to prepare historic contexts or thematic frameworks addressing these histories is certainly an important starting point. But keeping preservation relevant within all of these communities will require an even more intentional set of outreach strategies, meaningful collaborations with community-based organizations, and sophisticated, multilingual communication.

In particular, OHR has acknowledged that it needs to pursue funding to identify and preserve significant places associated with the indigenous communities of Los Angeles and Southern California. Many of these historic resources may not be part of the extant built environment that has represented the focus of traditional historic preservation efforts. A renewed focus on the heritage of the region's native peoples will require an initial framework through the development of a historic context statement, as well as more specialized city government expertise in archeological resources.

THE WATTS TOWERS, THE SINGULAR ARTISTIC VISION OF ITALIAN-AMERICAN IMMIGRANT SABATO "SIMON" RODIA, ANCHORS A CULTURALLY VIBRANT DISTRICT OF TANGIBLE AND INTANGIBLE HERITAGE WITHIN THE WATTS COMMUNITY.

PRESERVATION AND SYSTEMIC RACISM

In 2020, the acts of violence that took the lives of George Floyd, Ahmaud Arbery, Breonna Taylor, and countless other Black Americans led to a watershed moment in the fight against systemic racism. The Black Lives Matter movement and the national conversation around racial justice began to spur a parallel conversation about the role historic preservation has played in reinforcing racist practices and outcomes.

As books such as Richard Rothstein's *The Color of Law* and many others have documented, land use policies and zoning practices over many decades have institutionalized and reinforced racial segregation, wealth disparities, environmental injustice, and financial disinvestment in communities of color across the nation. Since historic preservation is an important subset of these planning and land use practices, all of our preservation policies should be reexamined through the lens of racial equity.

Historic preservation advocates and professionals have begun to listen more deeply and openly, to self-reflect critically, and to recommit to serving all communities in a manner that promotes equity and inclusivity. But there is much more to be done.

A disproportionately small percentage of historic preservation professionals and advocates represent communities of color, creating a homogeneity within the field that may perpetuate conscious or unconscious biases. Our landmark designation programs have also fallen short: despite OHR's efforts to create more diverse preservation frameworks through SurveyLA, fewer than 5 percent of Los Angeles's designated Historic-Cultural Monuments reflect associations with the city's BIPOC (Black, Indigenous, and Persons of Color) communities. In part, this reflects a decades-long legacy of a historic nomination process that has always been democratic and open to all—but can therefore end up privileging those who have the most time and resources to research and submit nominations. Preservation programs have also traditionally relied on written documentation, disadvantaging communities that have passed down their histories orally, or that have received less attention from researchers.

Rectifying these inequities will require concerted attention, along with dedication of new financial resources. It will mean re-examining traditional historic preservation standards to consider whether they are creating undue burdens on communities of color; providing more technical assistance to residents who lack the financial means to retain historic preservation architects or consultants for rehabilitation projects; re-examining hiring practices in preservation organizations as well as equity and access in the profession's educational pipeline; and more consistently advancing nominations that will help rectify the disparities in who is represented by the historic resources that get designated.

These re-examinations should also resist blanket criticisms and instead embrace the nuance and complexity of today's preservation realities. For example, local historic districts have been critiqued as consistently perpetuating inequitable land use patterns originally established through racially restrictive covenants. While this may sometimes be accurate, the most vigorous advocacy to create new historic districts (HPOZs) in Los Angeles has been emerging from majority African American neighborhoods. Many of these residents cherish the communities they have built over many decades, and see historic district status as the best protection against both economic displacement and cultural erasure.

CHINATOWN, WITH CENTRAL PLAZA AS ITS HEART, IS ONE OF MANY L.A. COMMUNITIES WHERE CULTURAL PRESERVATION STRATEGIES CAN BUILD UPON TRADITIONAL HISTORIC PRESERVATION TOOLS.

PEOPLE-CENTERED PRESERVATION

Creating a more equitable historic preservation movement will likely also require expanding the preservation toolkit, focusing not only on brick and mortar, but also on the people and lived experiences that help define cultural heritage.

The traditional tools of preservation are not always sufficient to help communities identify and protect what makes their cultural heritage unique. Historic designations, such as local landmark or historic district programs, help prevent demolitions or insensitive alterations of buildings and places. But they do not always help retain in place the people who inhabit those spaces, nor do they safeguard a community's intangible heritage, such as food, cultural practices, or customs.

Increasingly, Los Angeles's historic designations

have included cases where this disconnect has become more visible. For example, the Historic-Cultural Monument designation of the Johannes Brothers Building in the Arts District, near Little Tokyo, did not prevent the displacement of Japanese American artists who had made the building one of the earliest live/work complexes for Downtown artists. The HCM designation of the Bob Baker Marionette Theater helped protect its modest building, but could not protect the on-site cultural practice of puppeteering: as the property was being redeveloped for new housing, the theater troupe decided to relocate several miles away, to Highland Park.

Los Angeles may need to develop new tools that reflect preservation of cultural practices, such as the idea of "Cultural Districts," which have been pioneered in San Francisco. Such districts aim to preserve intangible

INTERIOR OF PANN'S, A LEGACY BUSINESS
OPERATING IN WESTCHESTER SINCE 1958

heritage or "living heritage" by identifying the activities that occur in these areas, such as services, foods, events, and social practices. Cultural Districts do not typically involve regulation of demolitions or design review for new permits, but instead emphasize marketing, technical assistance, and economic development efforts to preserve and promote key cultural practices.

Los Angeles has been exploring another San Francisco initiative to help sustain "legacy businesses" in communities. SurveyLA helped identify many of these businesses, with histories stretching back several decades, that have been integral to the identity of their local community. This work can serve as a starting point for a broader effort to create a legacy business registry that would help promote and financially support these important neighborhood cultural landmarks.

This people-centered focus also extends into the commemoration of our history through monuments and memorials. While Los Angeles may not have the Confederate monuments of Southern cities, monuments reflecting its Spanish Colonial legacy, such as the Father Junipero Serra statue at El Pueblo, have become sites of contention. Painful historic episodes, such as the 1871 Chinese Massacre in which nineteen Chinese American men were killed, lack any meaningful public memorial. The city's Civic Memory Working Group, convened in 2020 by Mayor Eric Garcetti and his chief design officer, former *Los Angeles Times* architecture critic Christopher Hawthorne, has made a set of recommendations to develop more thoughtful, equitable, and community-based processes that will help guide the memorialization and interpretation of forgotten or erased histories of Los Angeles.

In all of these ways, and many others, historic preservation's next chapter is starting to move beyond a single-minded focus on architecture and buildings to encompass approaches that put people first—a concept that the National Trust for Historic Preservation embraced in a 2017 report, "Preservation for People: A Vision for the Future." Traditional preservation tools such as historic district designation will likely become part of a broader toolkit, involving a more inclusive approach to cultural preservation that can also address interpretation of historic sites, mapping of a community's tangible and intangible cultural assets, a focus on civic memory and commemoration, and attention to equitable new development.

With SurveyLA and its past historic preservation successes as a solid starting point, Los Angeles is well-poised to develop such a people-centered preservation ethic. These shifts, together with new opportunities to synthesize historic preservation with affordable housing, the urgent climate challenge, and racial equity, can create the next generation of historic preservation success stories for Los Angeles—and for all of America's communities.

THE LEIMERT PARK VILLAGE "PEOPLE STREET" PLAZA, ON 43RD PLACE IN FRONT OF THE HISTORIC VISION THEATRE, PROVIDES AN ACTIVE GATHERING PLACE FOR A NEIGHBORHOOD WITH DISTINCTIVE AFRICAN AMERICAN CULTURAL ASSETS.

AFTERWORD
THE AMERICAN CITY AFTER COVID-19

As this book went to press, Los Angeles and other U.S. cities remained in the throes of the global COVID-19 pandemic, as well as its accompanying economic crisis. Across Los Angeles, the historic buildings and neighborhoods that had been vibrant economic generators or places of gathering and community suddenly became shuttered and quiet.

As Los Angeles began to emerge from its shutdown, local communities found that many of their cherished legacy businesses and established uses in historic buildings were simply not going to return. These jarring dislocations left us all to wonder: What would a post-pandemic Los Angeles look like?

The answer may come back to one of this book's themes—that while historic preservation is not a way of stopping change, it's our best method of managing change.

Los Angeles has faced sudden, daunting physical change many times in the past, from devastating earthquakes and fires fueled by Santa Ana winds, to the fires of civil unrest. This time, the rubble left behind is more figurative than literal; the buildings remain standing, even if the city's vitality and soul is sapped.

Lessons learned in Los Angeles about the value of historic preservation during previous periods of change can offer a source of strength not just for this city, but for all cities re-emerging from the pandemic. At a time when America's common bonds seem increasingly frayed, historic preservation offers a built-in sense of community and connection. The resilience and social cohesion found naturally in historic neighborhoods can provide a firm base from which our communities can rebound. During the Los Angeles stay-at-home orders, community leaders in historic districts partnered with the Office of Historic Resources to create self-made, cellphone-shot virtual walking tours, sharing their love for their historic neighborhoods with the rest of the city online during the challenging times of social distancing.

At a time when communities are grappling with how best to create jobs, historic preservation offers time-tested strategies that support economic vitality. Every dollar spent on historic rehabilitation instead of new construction generates more jobs and more local income, creating a powerful local economic multiplier effect. It's no accident that the most economically vibrant districts in Los Angeles prior to the pandemic also had high concentrations of historic resources—as new or growing businesses were increasingly seeking out places of authenticity and character.

At a time when communities are striving to build upon the reductions in carbon emissions achieved during social distancing, the reuse and energy retrofitting of historic buildings offers the most sustainable path to recovery, helping to prevent a slower-moving catastrophe from engulfing our planet.

And at a time when communities are feeling a sense of erasure, losing places or experiences we once loved, historic preservation provides the most effective way to keep us connected to the places and stories that enduringly define our city. As we feel somewhat adrift in an increasingly unfamiliar urban landscape, historic preservation can anchor us, guiding us to what we still want to hold onto firmly in our communities while also helping us see more clearly where dramatically transformative change may be possible.

Just as historic preservation tapped into deep-seated human needs for community, authenticity, and continuity to create a more vibrant city before the pandemic, so it can also become the source of a post-COVID urban renaissance.

SANCTUARY OF
CONGREGATIONAL
CHURCH OF NORTHRIDGE,
9659 BALBOA BLVD (1961),
DESIGNED BY A. QUINCY
JONES AND FREDERICK
EMMONS

APPENDIX
SURVEYLA DISCOVERIES

This field guide presents some of the interesting discoveries from SurveyLA—just a small sampling of what can be found in the city's comprehensive online inventory, HistoricPlacesLA, from many years of survey work across Los Angeles. Since the surveys were completed in each of the city's thirty-five Community Plan Areas, the findings are presented here in these same geographies.

While many sites that the Office of Historic Resources helps to preserve have attained iconic status, few of the places identified in the survey were widely known previously. SurveyLA has expanded the canon of significant Los Angeles architecture: numerous architects featured in these discoveries, including Richard Dorman, Sidney Eisenshtat, Harry Gesner, and Kemper Nomland Jr., are deserving of more focused research or monographs of their work. And many of the discoveries also extend well beyond architectural significance, reflecting important historic places that speak to each community's social and cultural history.

A key takeaway for all who participated in SurveyLA, day after day, was that every community in Los Angeles has significant architecture and cultural history worth identifying and celebrating.

CANOGA PARK × WINNETKA × WOODLAND HILLS × WEST HILLS

■ **4242 Elzevir Rd., Woodland Hills** (1926), a rare intact example of a 1920s building associated with the early community of Girard, the vision of developer Victor Girard, which predated today's Woodland Hills.

■ **The Eastwood Estates/Fieldstone Series Historic District** (1955), consisting of thirty-six parcels in Woodland Hills, located on the west and east sides of Jumilla Avenue above Delano Street with adjacent parcels on the west side of Corbin Avenue. It is an excellent example of a Mid-Century Modern postwar suburban subdivision, designed by noted architects Palmer and Krisel, who were best known for their "Alexander Homes" in Palm Springs, developed in the late 1950s and early 1960s by George and Robert Alexander, which have become synonymous with upscale Modernist living.

■ **20117 Stagg St., Winnetka** (1924), one of seven surviving examples identified in the survey of rare, early San Fernando Valley farmhouses from Winnetka's Charles Weeks Poultry Colony, a utopian agricultural community between 1923 and 1934, in which property owners raised chickens on their one-acre properties for egg production, sales, and distribution.

◼ **Crippled Children's Society of Southern California,** 6560 Winnetka Ave., Woodland Hills (1979), a Late Modern/ Expressionist building that is a late work of master architect John Lautner, saved in 2016 from potential demolition and converted to the nation's first Israeli-American community center.

◼ **Epiphany Lutheran Church,** 7769 Topanga Canyon Blvd., Canoga Park (1959), an outstanding example of a Mid-Century Modern ecclesiastical structure, designed by architect Edward Davies, with a soaring A-frame chapel.

◻ **Canoga Park Post Office,** 21801 Sherman Way, Canoga Park (1939), an excellent example of a PWA Moderne post office.

◼ **7014 Eton Ave., Canoga Park** (1929), a Craftsman home that is a rare West Valley example of a "shotgun" house (in which all rooms directly align, front to back).

■ **Liberace House,** 15405 Valley Vista Blvd., Encino (1953), the property most associated with the productive life of popular mid-twentieth century entertainer Liberace; the house was designed and constructed specifically for Liberace, with a piano-shaped swimming pool and a balustrade ornamented with musical bars and notes.

■ **5300 Amestoy Ave., Encino** (1935), an early Hacienda-style custom ranch house in the San Fernando Valley, with high-quality design.

■ **4821 Encino Terrace, Encino** (1968), an excellent example of Mid-Century Modern residential architecture, designed by architect Barry Gittelson.

■ **Fleetwood Center,** 19613 Ventura Blvd., Tarzana (1987), a rare example of Mimetic or Programmatic architecture; the building's design mimics the front of a 1970s Fleetwood Cadillac.

ENCINO × TARZANA

■ **Bothwell Ranch,** 5300 Oakdale Ave., Tarzana (1926), an intact thirteen-acre citrus orchard that is one of the last remaining commercial orchards in the San Fernando Valley, continuously in operation by the Bothwell family from 1926 to 2019.

▨ **Edgar Rice Burroughs, Inc.,** 18358 Ventura Blvd., Tarzana (1927), a Spanish Colonial Revival building significant for its association with Edgar Rice Burroughs, noted author of the *Tarzan* novels and developer of Tarzana. This was Edgar Rice Burroughs's office, continues to be the home of Edgar Rice Burroughs, Inc., and appears to be the only remaining building associated with Burroughs, as his Tarzana residence has been demolished.

▨ **Walter Leimert Real Estate Office,** 19130 Ventura Blvd., Tarzana, a real estate building for developer Walter Leimert built at another location and moved to this property in 1949. The building served as a popular local business until the 1990s; it was saved from demolition by the local community and turned into a Tarzana community/cultural center.

RESEDA × WEST VAN NUYS

■ **Sven Lokrantz Special Education Center,** 19451 Wyandotte St., Reseda (1961), an excellent example of Mid-Century Modern institutional architecture, designed by notable local architect Sidney Eisenshtat. The school, named for the founder of corrective physical education in America, has employed innovative educational methods to help students with physical disabilities.

■ **Reseda Theater,** 18447 Sherman Way in Reseda (1948), a significant 1940s neighborhood movie theater designed by the notable theater architect S. Charles Lee, who was also responsible for the Los Angeles Theatre on Broadway and other movie palaces. Vacant and boarded up since 1988, the theater has been slated for rehabilitation as part of a proposed mixed-use project that aims to revitalize the Sherman Way corridor.

■ **18240 Erwin St., Reseda** (1911), an American Foursquare-style home that is a rare, remaining example of an early farm house in Reseda.

■ **Tahitian Village,** 7923 Reseda Blvd., Reseda (1964), a courtyard apartment with distinctive features of the Tiki-Polynesian style.

■ **Sound City Studios,** 15464 W. Cabrito Rd., West Van Nuys (1965), significant as the founding and long-term location of Sound City Studios, an important recording studio in the history of rock music. Notable artists such as Fleetwood Mac, Nirvana, and Neil Young recorded albums at this location.

▨ **Anheuser-Busch Brewery,** 15800 Roscoe Blvd., West Van Nuys (1954), a 95-acre property with numerous industrial buildings and structures used in the brewing, bottling, storage, and shipping of Budweiser beer. The brewery includes a 1954 Mid-Century Modern administration building, from which tours are given. From 1966 to 1977, the site included the 17-acre Busch Gardens amusement park, complete with a bird sanctuary, monorail, boat rides, bumper cars, and free beer with admission.

▨ **Birmingham General Hospital** (bounded by Vanowen Street, Victory Boulevard, Aldea Avenue, and Balboa Boulevard), West Van Nuys (1944), a World War II hospital that was the US Army's most advanced center for the treatment of quadriplegic and paraplegic veterans. Prior to the hospital's closing in 1950, Marlon Brando shot his first film, *The Men*, on the property. In 1953, the Los Angeles Unified School District began using the property for Birmingham Junior High School (later, Birmingham High School and other school campuses).

■ **10739 Kling St., North Hollywood** (1907), a rare remaining example of a grandly scaled, early 1900s Craftsman residence in North Hollywood, dating to the earliest period of North Hollywood's residential development, before it was consolidated into the City of Los Angeles.

■ **10720 Camarillo St., North Hollywood** (1941), a Streamline Moderne fourplex designed by architect Carl Kay, conveying high-quality design and craftsmanship.

■ **Department of Water and Power Receiving Station E,** 5740 Whitnall Hwy., North Hollywood (1938), a PWA Moderne receiving station with Art Deco and Egyptian Revival elements, representing the 1930s expansion of municipal services in the East San Fernando Valley.

■ **Rancho Vega Garden Apartments,** 10559 Edison Way, North Hollywood (1945), a large World War II-era garden apartment complex designed by Paul R. Williams as housing for workers at the nearby Lockheed-Vega aircraft plant during World War II. The apartments are built in a 10.3-acre super-block with twenty-three residential buildings, with common courtyards, concrete walkways, and an emphasis on landscape. It is a rare intact example of local wartime defense worker housing and highlights Williams's interest in the social benefits of "garden city" planning principles for residents of multi-family housing.

■ **North Hollywood Masonic Lodge,** 5124 Tujunga Ave., North Hollywood (1949), a postwar Masonic lodge significant for its Exotic Revival architecture, with elements of Mayan Revival. It was designed by Robert Stacey-Judd, a preeminent architect of the Mayan Revival style, in collaboration with lodge member John Aleck Murrey. The lodge continues to occupy the building, which was designated as Historic-Cultural Monument #1078 in 2015, following its identification in the survey.

■ **Valley Federal Bank Tower/Los Angeles Federal Savings and Loan Association,** 12160 Victory Blvd., North Hollywood (1960), one of only a few high-rise corporate towers constructed in the San Fernando Valley at the time, built soon after the 1957 repeal of the city's 150-foot height limit. Located adjacent to the Valley Plaza shopping center and one of the first modern shopping centers in the nation, it was designed by significant postwar architects Honnold and Rex in the Corporate International Style.

■ **Circus Liquor,** 5606 Vineland Ave., North Hollywood (1959), significant as a longtime Valley business, the flagship location for a small chain of Valley liquor stores that use the iconic clown figure featured in the sign at this location. The business and sign have been featured in numerous films and television shows, becoming a San Fernando Valley visual landmark.

Magnolia and Whitsett Commercial Historic District, Valley Village, a block-long commercial corridor of five buildings on both sides of Magnolia Avenue between Whitsett Avenue and Wilkinson Avenue. Developed between 1934 and 1953, the buildings are one story, designed in a commercial interpretation of the Tudor Revival with fantasy decorative elements. Valley Photo Service has occupied the same location at the southeast corner of Whitsett and Magnolia since 1952, and features a mural along its Whitsett façade.

Sunkist Headquarters Building, 14130 Riverside Dr., Sherman Oaks (1970), notable for both its Brutalist corporate architecture, designed by master architects Albert C. Martin and Associates, and as the iconic headquarters of Sunkist Corporation, whose history is closely linked to the citrus heritage of the San Fernando Valley.

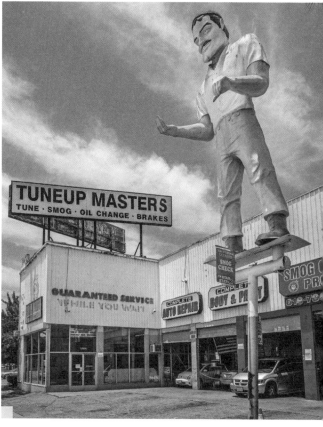

■ **14205 Hamlin St., Van Nuys** (1913), a Craftsman/Airplane Bungalow home that is a rare remaining example of a residence from Van Nuys's first few years of settlement; the home's chimney and porch were replaced after the 1994 Northridge Earthquake.

■ **Van Nuys Muffler Man,** 15237 Sherman Way, Van Nuys (1969), a striking freestanding painted fiberglass Muffler Man advertising what is now a smog check and tune-up shop.

■ **Horace Heidt's Magnolia Estates Apartments,** 14130 Magnolia Blvd. (1957; second phase in 1964), significant as an unusual example of a 1950–1960s garden apartment complex with a unified plan, featuring multiple buildings, swimming pools, tennis courts, and a clubhouse. The complex retains a whimsical design with Tiki/ Polynesian elements, including volcanic rock, waterfalls, tropical foliage (palm trees), decorative structures, a miniature golf course, and directional signs. The property was owned and designed by renowned bandleader Horace Heidt and was modeled after hotels in Palm Springs and Hawaii; the retired Heidt and some members of his band resided on site.

■ **Cameron Woods Estates Residential Historic District** (1947–1951), Van Nuys, a block-long single-family residential historic district of thirty single-family homes located along Orion Avenue between Victory Boulevard and Erwin Street, mostly designed in the Traditional Ranch and American Colonial Ranch styles. The district's collection of Ranch-style houses with mature trees and traditional styles makes the neighborhood a popular location for film crews.

■ **Longridge Avenue-Atoll Avenue Residential Historic District, Sherman Oaks** (1951), a single-family residential district with thirty-four residences along Longridge Avenue, Atoll Avenue, and Huston Street, north of Riverside Drive and east of Fulton Avenue. The district is significant for its collection of Ranch-style residences in an early postwar suburb developed by William Mellenthin. Mellenthin was an influential developer in the San Fernando Valley, building numerous single-family homes during the 1950s; he is best known for his Traditional Ranch neighborhoods featuring houses with exaggerated dovecotes that earned his homes the nickname "birdhouses."

■ **The Lamplighter/Stanley Burke's/Corky's,** 5049 Van Nuys Blvd., North Sherman Oaks (1958), a striking Googie-style coffee shop designed by Armet and Davis, masters of this style.

■ **11222 Dilling St.** (1959), a contemporary ranch house that was used as the exterior for the Brady residence on the *Brady Bunch* television series (1969–1974); the house was purchased and renovated by HGTV in 2019, transforming the inside of the house to match the Brady family interiors originally created on a soundstage set.

■ **Casa de Cadillac/Don Lee Cadillac,** 14401 Ventura Blvd., Sherman Oaks (1949), a striking application of Mid-Century Modernism to commercial architecture with eye-catching neon signage, all designed by noted architect Randall Duell, who was an art director at MGM Studios from 1937 to 1959 and designer of the Avalon Casino.

■ **3461 Cody Rd., Sherman Oaks** (1956), an excellent example of Mid-Century Modern post-and-beam residential architecture, designed by master architect Edward Fickett.

■ **Studio City Theatre**, 12136 Ventura Blvd., Studio City (1938), an extant 1930s neighborhood movie theater originally built for Fox Studios, designed by well-known theater architect Clifford A. Balch and converted to a bookstore in 1991.

■ **Stevens-Harnell House**, 3692 Berry Dr., Studio City (1985), one of the few post-1980 buildings captured in SurveyLA, an unusually distinctive Late Modern residence with Expressionist details designed by noted Portland-based architect Robert Harvey Oshatz.

■ **7110 Sycamore Trail, Cahuenga Pass** (1927), a unique folk art environment on a residential property. Originally constructed as a Spanish Colonial Revival house in 1927, this residence was purchased in 1967 by George Ehling, who transformed it over the next four decades into the "Tile House," covered throughout the interior and exterior with elaborate mosaics made of repurposed materials including ceramic, porcelain, marble, clay, glass bottles, and other found objects. Ehling also created a "dungeon apartment" lined with river rocks excavated from his backyard.

■ **The Boathouse Thematic Group** (1959), a unique example of hillside residential design and technological engineering innovation along the south side of the Cahuenga Pass. This grouping is composed of twelve identical single-family residences occupying steep, narrow hillside lots on Woodrow Wilson Drive and Pacific View Drive. With the hillside descending steeply toward the rear of the parcels, the residences are perched upon pier supports. These residences were designed by self-taught architect Harry Gesner, who hired a team of Norwegian shipbuilders to assist in the construction, using axes rather than saws for cutting wood to help achieve a handcrafted look.

■ **Amelia Earhart Residence,** 10042 Valley Spring Ln., Toluca Lake (1934), home of pioneer aviatrix Amelia Earhart and her husband, publisher George P. Putnam; Earhart lived here while preparing for her around-the-world flight that began in 1937.

■ **Barris Custom City,** 10807 Riverside Dr., Toluca Lake (1950), the long-term business of George Barris, the "King of Kustomizers," who died in 2015; Barris and his designers have designed and modified vehicles for film and television at this location since the early 1960s, including the *Batmobile*, General Lee in *The Dukes of Hazzard*, and the truck in *The Beverly Hillbillies*.

ARLETA × PACOIMA

■ **Calvary Baptist Church,** 12928 Vaughn St., Pacoima (1957), significant for its importance to the African American community in the San Fernando Valley and its association with Reverend Hillery T. Broadous, who founded the church in 1955 and played a large part in breaking down the Valley's racially restrictive covenants and segregation. The church was the site of NAACP rallies during the Civil Rights Movement, including a massive rally in 1965 featuring participants of the Selma-Birmingham Freedom March, and continues to host major community events.

■ **Ritchie Valens House,** 13428 Remington St., Pacoima (1947), a Minimal Traditional house that was the residence of nationally acclaimed rock and roll musician Ritchie Valens. Valens purchased the home for his mother in 1958 and resided here during the height of his professional career, until his death in 1959.

■ **Greater Community Baptist Church,** 11066 Norris Ave., Pacoima (1958), significant for its association with the Reverend T.G. Pledger, who founded the first African American church in the San Fernando Valley in 1942. Constructed in 1945 and rebuilt in 1958, the church played a significant role in the emergence of the fair housing movement in the San Fernando Valley and was the gathering place for significant community events and rallies during the 1960s and 1970s.

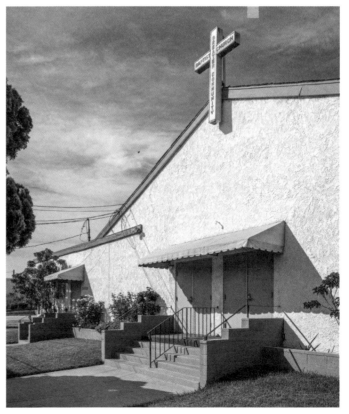

■ **Tip Top Hamburgers,** 8634 Woodman Ave., Arleta (1965), a distinctive example of a 1960s food stand, which was a significant component of the commercial landscape in the San Fernando Valley.

■ **San Fernando Valley Hongwanji Buddhist Temple,** 9450 Remick Ave., Arleta (1961), the first permanent Buddhist temple located in the San Fernando Valley, reflecting the diversity of Pacoima and the growth of a sizable Japanese American population in the area during the post-World War II era.

■ **13331 Fillmore St., Pacoima** (1932), an intact, early arroyo stone house distinctive for its use of regional materials.

■ **Merle Norman Cosmetics/ Nethercutt Collection,** a cluster of three industrial buildings at 15170–15200 Bledsoe St., which includes two single-story industrial buildings constructed for Merle Norman Cosmetics in 1958 and 1962; a four-story building constructed in 1970 houses one of the world's finest automobile collections assembled by the company's founder, J.B. Nethercutt.

The Nethercutt Collection opened to the public in 1971.

■ **Second Los Angeles Aqueduct,** 17001 Foothill Blvd., completed in 1970 at an estimated cost of $89 million; this aqueduct is 137 miles long with a capacity for 290,000 cubic feet of water. The new aqueduct supplemented the original Los Angeles Aqueduct (1913), which is already a Los Angeles Historic-

Cultural Monument; together, the two aqueducts supply about 70% of the city's water supply in most years.

■ **4-H Club,** 13514 Norris Ave., Sylmar (1946), an early agriculture-related industrial property associated with the 4-H Club, a youth development organization focused on developing agricultural skills.

SYLMAR

■ **M. Pfeifer Residence,** 13393 Gladstone Ave. (1936), a good representation of American Colonial Revival architecture, with Craftsman influence and arroyo stone features. It is the work of noted Los Angeles architect Peter K. Schabarum, who also designed Van Nuys City Hall.

■ **Sylmar Recreation Center,** 13181 Borden Ave. (1961), a public pool and two Mid-Century Modern buildings with folded plate roofs, designed by architects Deasy and Bolling.

■ **15101–15109 Roxford St. Bungalow Court** (1930–1933), five detached, single-story residential buildings with a central paved driveway; three are designed in the Spanish Colonial Revival style. The property may have been used as housing for relatives visiting patients at the nearby Olive View Sanatorium.

■ **Thomas C. Regan Studios,** 13553 Reedley St., Panorama City (1925), a silent movie studio that was among the earliest motion picture production facilities constructed in the San Fernando Valley; now occupied by American Legion Post 817, it is an unusually intact 1920s movie studio.

■ **9337 Sophia Ave., North Hills** (1956), one of the significant homes identified within the Storybook Village development, designed by noted Mid-Century Modern architects Palmer and Krisel, a neighborhood bounded by Plummer Street to the north, Tupper Street to the south, Debra Avenue to the west, and Swinton and Valjean Avenues to the east.

■ **Bear Pit BBQ,** 10825 Sepulveda Blvd., Mission HIlls (1958), a restaurant significant as the long-term location of a business important to the commercial identity of Mission Hills.

■ **Panorama Tower,** 8155 Van Nuys Blvd., Panorama City (1962), one of the San Fernando Valley's earliest commercial towers, designed in the Corporate International style by the significant Los Angeles architectural firm Welton Becket and Associates.

■ **Great Western Savings Bank,** 8201 Van Nuys Blvd., Panorama City (1957), an eye-catching example of Expressionist architecture designed by significant Los Angeles architect W.A. Sarmiento.

■ **Taos West Apartments,** 7924 Woodman Ave., Panorama City(1971), a complex that incorporates elements of the architectural vocabulary of Taos Pueblo in New Mexico and significant as a residential development designed and initially owned by actress Jane Russell, who grew up in the Panorama City area.

■ **Panorama Theater,** 9110 Van Nuys Blvd., Panorama City (1949), significant as an early neighborhood movie theater associated with the early commercial development of Panorama City and designed by significant Los Angeles architect William Pereira.

■ **Congregational Church of Northridge,** 9659 Balboa Blvd. (1961), a Mid-Century Modern church that is the work of noted architects A. Quincy Jones and Frederick Emmons.

■ **8813 Canby Ave.** (1914), a Craftsman residence that is one of the few remaining structures associated with the early community of Zelzah in the 1910s.

■ **Living-Conditioned Homes Residential Historic District,** a residential neighborhood northeast of Devonshire Street and Reseda Boulevard, with fifty-three Mid-Century Modern homes designed by noted Los Angeles architects Palmer & Krisel. The neighborhood is the only Palmer & Krisel tract in the San Fernando Valley to exhibit the flamboyant characteristics most commonly associated with their "Alexander style" developments in Palm Springs and Las Vegas, aimed at bringing high-end Modernism to the masses.

■ **Chateau Highlands Residential Historic District,** a neighborhood of 131 residential properties generally bounded by Kinzie Street to the north, Plummer Street to the south, Vanalden Avenue to the east, and Tampa Avenue to the west. The district is composed of single-family Ranch-style houses developed between 1956 and 1963, sited on large, half-acre lots and custom-designed by a variety of builders and/or architects. The neighborhood offers an excellent concentration of Ranch-style architecture (mostly Traditional and Contemporary Ranches), with quality design and craftsmanship.

■ **Northridge Skateland,** 18140 Parthenia St. (1958), a vernacular commercial building that is one of the few extant Valley skating facilities; historically, it hosted dance nights that attracted such celebrity acts as Ike and Tina Turner, Iron Butterfly, and the Standells. Notably, it was also one of very few commercial venues in the Valley where African Americans congregated regularly during the era of the civil rights movement.

■ **19224 Superior St.** (1961), a custom-designed Contemporary Ranch home notable for its dramatic roofline and quality craftsmanship.

■ **Roy Rogers and Dale Evans Residence,** 22832 Trigger St., Chatsworth (1938), significant as the former residence of renowned entertainment stars Roy Rogers and Dale Evans, who resided at this property between 1955 and 1965. While the house remains intact, much of the adjacent ranch was subdivided into a residential tract in the 1960s.

■ **Garden of the Gods,** an undeveloped site in northwest Chatsworth that includes a significant grouping of rock formations, located north of Santa Susana Pass Road near the base of the Santa Susana Mountains. The twenty-three-acre site was an iconic filming location for productions depicting the American West and various exotic locations, and is one of few remaining undeveloped areas of the former Iverson Movie Ranch, one of Southern California's most prolific filming locations between 1912 and the postwar era.

■ **Rancho San Antonio Boys Home,** 21000 Plummer St., Chatsworth (1938), an innovative boys' boarding school that has remained in continuous operation since 1938, created to provide a structured environment to address juvenile delinquency and known as the "Boys' Town of the West."

CHATSWORTH × PORTER RANCH

■ **Congregational Church of Chatsworth,** 20440 Lassen St., Chatsworth (1964), a distinctive Mid-Century Modern church notable for its Expressionist design features.

■ **Devonshire Highlands Historic District,** bounded by Kinzie Street to the north, Plummer Street to the south, Tampa Avenue to the east, and Tunney Avenue to the west, Northridge. This neighborhood of 111 residential properties was built between 1955 and 1964 and composed of distinctive, custom-designed Ranch-style houses sited on large, half-acre lots.

■ **Southern Pacific Railroad Tunnels No. 26, 27, and 28,** located northwest of Chatsworth Park South, west of Chatsworth Park North, and beneath Topanga Canyon Boulevard and Old Santa Susana Pass Road, respectively, Chatsworth. These three tunnels were excavated in 1904 through the Santa Susana Mountains as part of a railroad line that was an integral part of Southern Pacific's connection between Northern and Southern California.

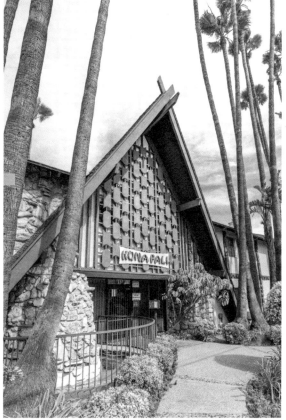

■ **11515 Shoshone Ave., Granada Hills** (1917), one of three bunkhouses that are remnants of the Sunshine Ranch, a 2,000-acre citrus ranch operated by M.H. Mosier from 1917 to 1925.

■ **St. Stephen's Lutheran Church,** 15950 Chatsworth St., Granada Hills (1966), an Expressionist design by noted church architects Orr, Strange, Inslee & Senefeld. The church features an art glass window composed of 14,000 pieces of glass, designed by Roger Darricarrere for the 1964 New York World's Fair.

■ **17410 Mayerling St., Granada Hills** (1887), a surprising nineteenth-century architectural presence with ornate Queen Anne residential design that was the work of noted architect Joseph Cather Newsom. Originally constructed in 1887 in Pacoima, this residence was moved to Granada Hills in the 1970s.

■ **Kona Pali Apartments,** 10520 Balboa Blvd. Granada Hills (1962), a skillful application of the Tiki-Polynesian style to multi-family residential architecture.

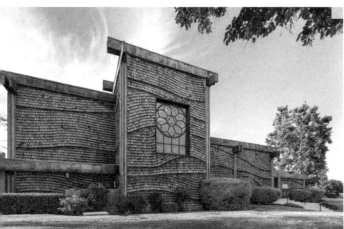

■ **Marlborough Palms Residential Historic District,** bounded generally by Chatsworth Street to the north, Debra Avenue to the east, San Jose Street to the south, and Hayvenhurst Avenue to the west, Granada Hills (1957–1958). A cohesive neighborhood of 149 homes in variations of the Ranch style, including Cinderella, Traditional, and Contemporary styles; sixty-five of the homes were designed by the architectural firm Palmer & Krisel.

■ **Episcopal Church of St. Andrews and St. Charles,** 16651 Rinaldi St., Granada Hills (1960), a Mid-Century Modern church designed by the noted church architect Carleton Winslow Jr.

■ **Woody's Smorgasburger/ International House of Pancakes (IHOP),** 16943 Devonshire St., Granada Hills (1962), a Googie-style commercial structure that was originally built as a Woody's Smorgasburger. Many Woody's locations were later converted into International House of Pancakes restaurants, to the extent that their distinctive A-frame rooflines and blue roof shingles are now most associated with IHOP.

■ **Pink Motel and Cadillac Jack's,** 9457–9475 San Fernando Rd., Sun Valley (1947, 1949), one of the best remaining examples of a roadside motel and coffee shop in the San Fernando Valley. The Pink Motel was constructed in 1947 by Joseph Thomulka; two years later Thomulka added the Pink Cafe, now called Cadillac Jack's. Designed in the Mid-Century Modern style, both buildings display a distinctive pink-and-blue paint scheme. At one time, there were many motels along this stretch of San Fernando Road (Route 99, extending into Northern California); most have been demolished or substantially altered. Today, the property is used exclusively as a filming location.

■ **Big Jim's Restaurant Sign,** 8950 Laurel Canyon Blvd., Sun Valley (1979), a noteworthy commercial neon pole sign depicting a cowboy riding a galloping horse.

■ **Dundee Egg Farms,** 7645–7649 San Fernando Rd., Sun Valley (1931), an intact remnant of the early industrial development along San Fernando Road in Sun Valley, associated with the San Fernando Valley's agricultural legacy. References to the original use include a cast stone egg above the entrance on the one-story portion of the building.

■ **Rodriguez Market,** 7806 Lemp Ave., Sun Valley (1930), a 1930s neighborhood market that appears to pre-date much of the surrounding development by several decades.

■ **Our Lady of Zapopan Chapel,** 7824 Lankershim Blvd., Sun Valley (1942), a 1940s Catholic church associated with the early Latino community of the Northeast Valley.

This Mission Revival style chapel was operated by Our Lady of the Holy Rosary parish in Sun Valley to serve local agricultural workers.

■ **10451 Penrose St., Shadow Hills** (1928), a residence that reflects the early residential development in Shadow Hills, incorporating local arroyo stone in its porch piers and chimney.

■ **Old Vienna Gardens,** 9955 Sunland Blvd., Shadow Hills (1934), an elaborate Moorish Revival-style residence built by August Furst, who had emigrated from Nuremberg, Germany, in the 1920s. Furst wanted to establish an "Old World" restaurant at the bottom of the hill. The Old Vienna Gardens restaurant, built in 1937, featured a whimsical design inspired by various European Revival styles including English Tudor and Swiss Chalet; the site now operates as Villa Terraza Italian restaurant. The surrounding grounds include hillside terracing, stairways, gardens, patios, and duck ponds—some of which were constructed of local arroyo stone.

■ **Hardin House,** 10226 Marcus Ave., Tujunga (1921), constructed using local arroyo stone and may have also been one of the earliest schools in the area, as a 1920s schoolhouse.

■ **Hotel Tujunga and "Sister Elsie's Well,"** 6720 St. Esteban St., Tujunga (1932). The Hotel Tujunga was constructed on property previously owned by Philip Begue, one of Tujunga's first residents. The hotel was designed around an arroyo stone well head, known as "Sister Elsie's Well," originally dug on the Rancho Las Hermanas, and named for a local nun who worked with displaced Native Americans during the early 1800s. Today, the property operates as Foothill Retirement, a senior-living facility.

SUNLAND × TUJUNGA

◼ **Sunair Asthma Home,** 7754–7770 McGroarty Ave., Tujunga (1937), established on this site in 1937 by pharmacist George S. Davis as the first live-in rehabilitation center of its kind. Davis was a half-owner of Parke-Davis Pharmaceutical Company, now known as Pfizer, which was once the world's largest pharmaceutical company. The original stonework was created by George Harris, a local stone mason who built many stone structures throughout Tujunga in the early twentieth century. The property, now occupied by the Smart Academy Christian School, retains numerous arroyo stone features, including retaining walls, steps, and planters.

◼ **Scott Exposed Steel House,** 10300 Haines Canyon Ave., Tujunga (1956), one of the earliest steel houses designed by Case Study architect Pierre Koenig, with steel post-and-beam construction, corrugated steel walls, and a curtain wall of windows.

◼ **Castle Hi-Yan-Ka,** 9936 Redmont Ave., Tujunga (1922), developed as the home of Mary and Ray Phillips. In 1922, Ray purchased a two-acre ranch and proceeded to build a garden that included staircases, a stone tower, outdoor fireplaces, and guest houses, all constructed of stones found on the property. Mary established a wildlife sanctuary and tourist attraction on the site, which by 1938 was also home to numerous wild birds. Ray later added rock-lined paths, grottos, fountains, and thousands of trees, shrubs, and flowers. Over time, the site drew over 100,000 visitors. The name "Hi-Yan-Ka" is derived from the Tujunga Native American language meaning "complete welcome."

BEL-AIR × BEVERLY CREST

■ **Judy Garland Residence,** 1231 Stone Canyon Rd., Bel-Air (1938), a Traditional Ranch house designed by Wallace Neff that was constructed for actress and singer Judy Garland, who lived here with her mother from 1938 to 1943, the period when she rose to stardom in the film *The Wizard of Oz.*

■ **1053 Stone Canyon Rd., Bel-Air** (1933), an American Colonial Ranch home designed by Gerard Colcord, who was a notable and prolific designer of estates for Hollywood society figures in the Bel-Air and Beverly Hills areas.

■ **100 Bel-Air Rd., Bel-Air** (1924), a Spanish Colonial Revival style building that originally housed the sales offices for the Bel-Air Estates subdivision and now houses the offices of the Bel-Air Association.

BEL-AIR ✕ BEVERLY CREST

■ **The Mansion,** 2451 Laurel Canyon Blvd., Laurel Canyon (1925), a residential estate with Mediterranean Revival architecture that is significant for its association with a remarkable succession of high-profile celebrities, including: Beatrice Houdini, widow of illusionist Harry Houdini (1920s); actor Errol Flynn (1930s–1940s); organized crime boss Benjamin "Bugsy" Siegel (1940s–1950s); and musician Jimi Hendrix (1960s).

■ **Hearn Residence,** 10511 Selkirk Ln., Beverly Glen (1952), a well-preserved residential work of architect Lloyd Wright (son of Frank Lloyd Wright).

■ **2266, 2291, and 2315 San Ysidro Dr., Beverly Crest** (1959–1960), three distinctive residential works of Mid-Century Modern architecture designed by Richard Dorman.

■ **Old Ranch Road Residential Historic District, Brentwood/ Sullivan Canyon**, a neighborhood that was planned and constructed by Cliff May for ranch-style, equestrian-oriented living, with expansive lots that followed the natural curve of the existing road, lush landscaping, mature oaks and sycamores, bridle paths, and room for individual stables and corrals. At the far north end of the road is the Mandalay Gate House at 2200 Old Ranch Rd.—site of Cliff May House No. 5 (a.k.a. "Mandalay"), the last personal home of Cliff May (demolished in 1994).

■ **1500 Old Oak Rd., Brentwood** (1938), the third home of master architect Cliff May, which most fully embodies May's design ideas. After May lived here with his family from 1938 to 1939, the house was opened to the public in 1940 as a demonstration model for his Riviera Ranch residential development. From 1983 to 1985, May designed an addition for a subsequent owner, actor Robert Wagner.

■ **Arnold Schoenberg Residence,** 116 N. Rockingham Ave. (1925), Brentwood, from 1936 to 1951, the home of Austrian composer and painter Arnold Schoenberg, who was an important member of the European Jewish émigré community that developed on Los Angeles's Westside during and after World War II.

BRENTWOOD × PACIFIC PALISADES

■ **Uplifters Historic District,** which encompasses forty-six parcels in Pacific Palisades' Rustic Canyon area, including streets with cobblestone retaining walls, lush natural landscaping with many mature trees, and a period wooden sign for "Uplifters Ranch" suspended over Latimer Road. The Uplifters were a selective social club that had grown out of the Los Angeles Athletic Club (LAAC), originating with LAAC member Harry Marston Haldeman and attracting prominent members such as Walt Disney, Busby Berkeley, and L. Frank Baum. The Uplifters' clubhouse now serves as the Rustic Canyon Recreation Center; it was designated a Historic-Cultural Monument in 1999. The former Uplifters cottages, many of which reverted to private ownership by the late 1930s, are now private residences.

■ **Thelma Todd's Sidewalk Café,** 17575 Pacific Coast Hwy., Pacific Palisades (1928), one of the earliest intact 1920s neighborhood commercial buildings in the area. The Spanish Colonial Revival building by noted Westside architect Mark Daniels, served as a shopping center for the nearby Castellammare housing development. In the early 1930s, actress Thelma Todd opened a restaurant on the ground floor of the building; she lived in an ocean view apartment on an upper floor, while an exclusive Hollywood club called Joya occupied the rest of the second floor.

■ **708 House/Moss Residence,** 708 El Medio Ave., Pacific Palisades, an excellent example of Post-Modern residential architecture and an important early work by master architect Eric Owen Moss; a 600-square-foot expansion and complete remodel of a 1948 Case Study House, completed between 1979 and 1982 for the architect and his family.

◼ **The Aurilla Kempton Residence,** 3734 S. Grandview Ave., Mar Vista (1906), a Craftsman home with Queen Anne influences that is the oldest extant residence in Mar Vista, located in Los Angeles's first gated community, the Ocean Park Heights tract atop Mar Vista Hill.

◻ **4308 Berryman Ave., Del Rey** (1922), which appears to be the only remnant building from the early 1920s Barnes City Wild Animal Circus and Zoo. Part of Barnes City, an incorporated city consolidated into the City of Los Angeles in 1926.

◻ **3744 S. Barrington Ave., Mar Vista** (1908), a distinctive Craftsman home built in Pasadena and relocated to Mar Vista in the mid-1920s.

PALMS × MAR VISTA × DEL REY

■ **Villa Fontana,** 3732 S. Mentone Ave., Palms (1961), a particularly noteworthy Dingbat-style apartment building, displaying many features typical of the style, including building name signage, accent tile panels, and applied "dingbat" ornamentation.

■ **The Chili Bowl,** 12244 W. Pico Blvd., Mar Vista(1931), a building designed to resemble a bowl of chili—a rare extant example of Programmatic architecture. This building may be the only remaining example of eighteen Chili Bowl restaurants constructed throughout the Los Angeles area by Arthur Whizin prior to 1933.

■ **The Colonial Corners Commercial Historic District, Mar Vista** (1948–1962), three single-story and two-story commercial buildings located at the intersection of Barrington Avenue and National Boulevard. The buildings were developed by noted horticulturist and nurseryman Paul Howard, who in the 1930s operated a highly successful nursery called California Flowerland at 3rd Street and La Brea Avenue in Los Angeles. Designed in the American Colonial Revival style, each building displays a similar but unique design, with Colonial columns and a double-height, eight-sided tower at the corner.

VENICE

■ **Lost Venice Canals Historic District,** a residential neighborhood containing 449 properties bounded by Innes Place to the west, Westminster Avenue, and Alhambra Court to the north, Venice Boulevard to the southeast, and Grand Avenue to the south. The district, largely built between 1904 and 1929, is significant for its unique planning and development; it is the original residential neighborhood planned by Venice of America founder Abbot Kinney, oriented around the original Venice canals. By 1929, with the canals increasingly seen as deteriorating and as obstacles to progress and the automobile, this neighborhood's canals were filled in and paved over.

■ **St. Mark's Hotel,** 19 E. Windward Ave. (1905), a Renaissance Revival structure that is one of the few original Venice arcade buildings, developed as part of Abbot Kinney's Venice of America development. This building is the oldest remaining hotel in Venice and also displays three of Venice's best-known murals. St. Mark's Hotel was a popular hangout for Los Angeles beatniks who congregated in Venice during the 1950s, including at the Venice West Café discussed in Chapter 1.

■ **Arthur Reese Residence,** 541 E. Santa Clara Ave. (1913), the longtime residence of the first African American to live and work in Venice. Arthur Reese came to Venice from New Orleans in 1905 to work as a janitor and built this home in the Oakwood neighborhood, later inviting his cousins, the Tabors, to join him in Venice. Irving Tabor would become the chauffeur for Venice-founder Abbot Kinney. Reese was also an artist and sculptor and ultimately became the unofficial town decorator, mostly known for decorating Mardi Gras-style parade floats.

VENICE

■ **Venice Gondola Building,** 200 E. Mildred Ave. (1913), a vernacular structure that served as the repair shop and storage facility for the Venice canal gondolas (the street to the rear of the building was formerly a canal). Other sources suggest this building was also used as a machine shop to repair Venice's popular amusement park rides.

■ **Eames Office,** 901 S. Abbot Kinney Blvd. (1912), served as the office for American designers Charles and Ray Eames from 1943 to 1988. From this location, the Eames duo made significant contributions to architecture, furniture design, industrial design, graphic design, fine art, and film. The building had previously served as the Bay Cities Garage.

■ **2-4-6-8 House,** 932 W. Amoroso Pl. (1979), an example of Postmodern/Deconstructivist residential architecture in Venice and one of the earliest designs by noted Los Angeles architects Thom Mayne and Michael Rotondi. This small, cube-shaped building, perched on top of concrete blocks, features one window on each façade, with 2x2, 4x4, 6x6, and 8x8 dimensions.

WESTCHESTER/PLAYA DEL REY

■ **Milliron's Department Store,** 8715 S. Sepulveda Blvd., Westchester (1948), one of the earliest post-World War II Mid-Century Modern department stores (now Kohl's), with an innovative rooftop parking system designed by architect Victor Gruen, a pioneer of the modern shopping mall.

▨ **6674 S. Vista del Mar, Westchester** (1956), a duplex originally constructed in 1956 and altered in 1977 by notable architect Eric Owen Moss (with James Stafford), in a project cited as Moss's first built work. The structure reinterprets Streamline Moderne architecture in a distinctive, playful Late Modern design, emphasizing the building's verticality.

▨ **7050 W. 85th St., Westchester** (1944), a home designed with distinctive features and landscaping associated with the Tiki-Polynesian style.

■ **Hughes Aircraft Employee Credit Union,** 8131 S. Barnsley Ave., Westchester (1968), a striking New Formalist financial building, designed by architect Perry Langston.

■ **Paseo del Rey Multi-Family Historic District, Playa del Rey,** north of LAX on a hilly plateau between Manchester Avenue and Westchester Parkway, encompasses thirty-four early-1960s, two-story apartment buildings with interior courtyards, featuring lush landscaping such as tropical plants, mature trees, and rough rock planters.

■ **Fritz B. Burns Residence,** 200 E. Waterview St., Playa del Rey (1921), a Mediterranean Revival home that is significant as the residence of builder/developer Fritz B. Burns, who, with his Dickinson and Gillespie development firm, was responsible for the initial development of Playa del Rey. Burns lost this house to foreclosure after the 1929 Stock Market Crash, but went on to become one of the most important Los Angeles real estate developers of the post-World War II era.

WESTWOOD

■ **El Paseo,** 1001 S. Broxton Ave. (1931), an elegant Spanish Colonial Revival commercial development in Westwood Village; associated with the original development of Westwood by the Janss Corporation.

■ **Westwood Holmby Building/ Holmby Hall,** 901 Westwood Blvd. (1929), a Mediterranean Revival commercial building associated with the original development of Westwood by the Janss Investment Company and the work of master architect Gordon B. Kaufmann. Originally, the upper stories served as the first women's dormitory for UCLA students, called Holmby Hall. The building was rehabilitated in the 1980s, and the original clock tower was reconstructed in 2003 following a fire.

■ **Bullock's Department Store,** 1000 Westwood Blvd. (1932), the original Westwood Bullock's department store, designed by significant Los Angeles architects Parkinson & Parkinson.

WESTWOOD

▨ **Van Cleef House,** 651 S. Warner Ave. (1942), a Mid-Century Modern residence designed by Richard Neutra.

■ **Amelita Galli-Curci House,** 201 S. Tilden Ave. (1936), a Spanish Colonial Revival home designed by master architect Wallace Neff and noted landscape architects Florence Yoch and Lucille Council. The residence was constructed for the Italian opera singer Amelita Galli-Curci, for whom Neff built four houses over several years.

▨ **Comstock Hills Residential Historic District,** a residential subdivision with 307 properties roughly bounded by Santa Monica Boulevard, Beverly Glen Boulevard, Devon Avenue, Ashton and Comstock Avenues, and the Los Angeles Country Club. Original residences were constructed primarily from the 1920s through the 1950s, and designed in a variety of Period Revival styles, as well as Mid-Century Modern, Minimal Traditional, and Ranch styles. The neighborhood represents suburban residential planning from the early automobile era, developed by the influential Janss Investment Company beginning in 1922.

WEST LOS ANGELES

■ **La Lomita Ranch,** 2851 Overland Ave. (1925), an American Colonial Revival structure that is a surviving example of an early residential estate in West Los Angeles, now part of Notre Dame Academy.

▨ **2103 S. Colby Ave.** (1908), a Craftsman/Folk Victorian house built in Sawtelle well before that city was consolidated into the City of Los Angeles in 1922; the house remains mostly unaltered, though not maintained.

▨ **O.K. Nurseries/Hashimoto Nursery,** 1935 S. Sawtelle Blvd. (1928), a longstanding local business that is one of the last remaining Japanese American nurseries in this community—second only to Little Tokyo as a significant Japanese American commercial center in Los Angeles.

■ **National Boulevard Apartments,** 10565 National Blvd. (1954), a Mid-Century Modern complex that is an early work of architect Ray Kappe, adjacent to a 1955 garden apartment complex designed by Carl Maston.

■ **1180 S. Beverly Dr.** (1966), one of the most notable examples of Brutalist-style commercial architecture in Los Angeles, designed by Kurt Meyer and Associates for Liberty Savings and Loan.

■ **Johnson's Buffet,** 10275 W. Pico Blvd. (1932), a rare historic cafeteria (currently vacant) originally constructed to capitalize on the nearby, newly opened Fox Studios.

■ **Century Plaza Towers,** 2039 and 2049 Century Park East (1973), the twin towers in Century City designed by renowned architect Minoru Yamasaki; significant as an intact example of High Tech architecture (Structural Expressionism).

CENTRAL CITY (DOWNTOWN LOS ANGELES)

■ **White Log Coffee Shop,** 1061 S. Hill St. (1933), one of the few intact examples of Mimetic architecture in the city—a log cabin in Downtown Los Angeles designed by L.A. architects Norstrom and Anderson.

■ **Hotel Rosslyn,** 111 W. 5th St. (1914), an example of Beaux Arts commercial architecture that was once the largest hotel on the West Coast, designed by noted Los Angeles architects Parkinson and Bergstrom; includes a prominent neon rooftop sign.

■ **Continental Hotel,** 802 E. 7th St. (1912), significant for its history of providing low-cost accommodations to Chinese American laborers who were employed nearby at City Market, the city's wholesale produce center. This was one of relatively few residential hotels in the area that rented rooms to people of Chinese descent.

■ **Excelsior Steam Laundry,** 424 S. Los Angeles St. (1893), one of the oldest intact industrial buildings in the city, significant for its Romanesque Revival architecture and its role in labor history. In 1901, the predominantly female employees of Excelsior and six other steam laundries organized to form Local 52 of the Shirt Waist and Laundry Workers' International Union. The group advocated for a ten-hour work day and equal pay for women and men, culminating in a strike that marked a flashpoint in the local labor movement.

CENTRAL CITY (DOWNTOWN LOS ANGELES)

■ **Bendix Building,** 1206 S. Maple St. (1929), an early industrial loft designed to maximize available factory space vertically on a minimum amount of land. This building was constructed for the Bendix Corporation, a leading manufacturer of automobile and aircraft parts, and includes a neon rooftop sign. It is one of several Downtown buildings identified in the survey that is associated with Florence C. Casler, one of the first women active in Downtown real estate development. Casler is responsible for the design and development of prominent industrial buildings in what is now Downtown's Fashion District.

■ **Warner Bros. Downtown Theatre,** 411 W. 7th St. (1921), designed by noted architect B. Marcus Priteca and constructed as the second location of the Pantages Theatre. In 1929, the building was acquired by film titan Jack Warner and reopened as the Warner Bros. Downtown Theatre, remaining in operation as a motion picture theater until 1975. In recent decades, the former theater has become an anchor in Downtown's Jewelry District.

■ **Ville de Paris,** 420 W. 7th St. (1917), a Beaux Arts building designed by Dodd and Richards, constructed as the flagship location of Ville de Paris, a local department store.

CENTRAL CITY NORTH (CHINATOWN AND THE ARTS DISTRICT)

■ **Coca-Cola Syrup Manufacturing Plant,** 947 E. 4th Street, Arts District (1915), a factory in Downtown's primary industrial district, built by the internationally known Coca-Cola Company to produce syrup for its sodas. The building was substantially expanded and re-clad with its current design in 1939, by Coca-Cola's Atlanta-based architect Jesse M. Shelton.

■ **John A. Roebling's Sons Co.** (now Angel City Brewery), 216 S. Alameda St., Arts District (1913), which exhibits the features of a daylight factory building, designed

to maximize the amount of light reaching the interior of the building through bays of large industrial sash windows, skylights, and other roof forms that bring in additional light. The building was designed by master architects Hudson & Munsell, who were responsible for the Natural History Museum in Exposition Park, also in 1913.

■ **Canadian Hotel/Palace Hotel,** 712 E. Traction Ave., Arts District (1906), an early hotel building in Los Angeles. Known as the Canadian Hotel, it was built as a first-class hotel for African Americans, many of whom worked

as Pullman car porters, and was managed for its first five years by Canadian J.W. Gordon. From the 1970s through the 1990s it was the site of Al's Bar, an important gathering space in Los Angeles's Arts District that served as a "town square" for neighborhood artists. Al's Bar was opened in 1979 by local artist Marc Kreisel; he had purchased the space from the now-legendary Al, who had previously operated it as a truck-stop cafe. Al's Bar reached iconic status as the home of L.A.'s punk rock—and later grunge rock—scene before closing in 2001.

■ **Kim Ling Inn Restaurant/ Hop Sing Tong Benevolent Association,** 428 Gin Ling Way, Chinatown (1940), the longtime headquarters of an important Chinese benevolent association, whose Los Angeles chapter has been in operation since the 1890s. The group provides social welfare and cultural activities for Chinese immigrants, within a building of East Asian Eclectic design that once housed the Kim Ling Inn Restaurant.

■ **Golden Pagoda/Hop Louie's Jade Pagoda,** 946 Mei Ling Way, Chinatown (1940), a commercial building with East Asian Eclectic design that has been a longtime neighborhood barn. Originally known as Golden Pagoda, and then as Hop Louie's Jade Pagoda, it has been in continuous operation at this location since 1941.

■ **Cathay Bank,** 755 N. Broadway, Chinatown (1966), a commercial building designed by noted Chinese American architect Eugene Kinn Choy in a style blending New Formalism with simplified East Asian features, such as carved brackets and vertical signage. Cathay Bank was the first bank in Los Angeles to be operated by Chinese Americans.

■ **Macy Street School,** 505 E. Clara St., Downtown Los Angeles (1915), a Beaux Arts elementary school designed by master architect Albert C. Martin and a rare example of an LAUSD school building that predates the 1933 Long Beach Earthquake. It is significant for its association with Principal Nora Sterry, an important figure in the history of progressive education. Sterry implemented innovative educational and social programs from this school, designed to address the poverty, pollution, and unsanitary conditions in the surrounding neighborhood of recent immigrants, predominantly of Mexican and Chinese descent.

HOLLYWOOD

■ **Hollywoodland Realty,** 2700 N. Beachwood Dr. (1926), a Tudor Revival structure that was the original sales office for the Hollywoodland Realty Company, which erected the Hollywoodland Sign (later shortened to "Hollywood") atop the Hollywood Hills as a promotion built for the 1920s Hollywoodland residential development.

■ **Temple of the Vedanta Society,** 1946 N. Vedanta Pl. (1938), an Exotic Revival structure that applies Indian-inspired design elements to institutional architecture, with a distinctive onion dome.

■ **Canyon Country Store,** 2108 N. Laurel Canyon Blvd. (1924), a vernacular commercial structure that has operated as Laurel Canyon's neighborhood market and community gathering space since the 1920s. During the 1960s and 1970s, local musicians often met on the market's front patio to socialize and work on new songs together, in an era when Laurel Canyon residents included Joni Mitchell, Jim Morrison, David Crosby, Graham Nash, John and Michelle Phillips, and Cass Elliot.

■ **High Tower Elevator and Garages,** 2181 Broadview Ter. (1923), a free-standing elevator tower that provides access to hillside homes from the garages below; part of the original 1920s Alta Loma development, linked to a hillside network of concrete pedestrian stairways and walkways.

HOLLYWOOD

■ **Joseph Kun House No. 1,** 7960 W. Fareholm Dr. (1936), an important work of Early Modern residential architecture in the Hollywood Hills near Laurel Canyon, designed by Richard Neutra in collaboration with Gregory Ain.

■ **946–950 N. Martel Ave. Bungalow Court** (1924), one of several excellent examples of a 1920s bungalow court in Hollywood, designed in the Spanish Colonial Revival style.

■ **Television Center/Hollywood Technicolor Facility,** 6311 Romaine St. (1930), a massive Art Deco industrial building built to support Hollywood's film industry; it originally served as Technicolor's film processing plant and is now used as a television studio.

■ **221 N. Belmont Ave.** (1885), a Queen Anne-style house that reflects the earliest phase of residential development in Westlake.

▨ **Occidental Studios,** 201 N. Occidental Blvd. (1913), one of the oldest continuously operating motion picture studios in Los Angeles. Originally established as Bosworth Studios in 1913, the property was purchased by Adolph Zukor and Jesse Lasky and renamed Famous Players-Lasky-Morosco. During this period, Cecil B. DeMille, D.W. Griffith, and Mary Pickford were all affiliated with the studio, and Pickford lived in a house on the property. Now known as Occidental Studios, the property is one of the few extant studios that pre-dates the major studio era that began in the 1920s.

▨ **Los Angeles Pacific Railroad Substation,** 1147 Venice Blvd. (1903), a streetcar electric substation that exemplifies the early transit history of Los Angeles, originally constructed in 1903 for the Los Angeles Pacific Railroad Company.

WESTLAKE

■ **Azusa Street Revival** (Apostolic Faith Mission), 216 N. Bonnie Brae St. (1896), a Victorian Vernacular cottage that is significant as the birthplace of the modern Pentecostal movement in North America. In 1906, the residence was owned by John and Ruth Asberry and served as the original meeting place for what would become the Pentecostal Azusa Street Revival. African American preacher William Seymour, who began participating in services at this residence, is considered the founder of modern Pentecostalism, preaching until his death in 1922. His movement has now grown to more than 500 million followers.

■ **372 Laveta Ter.** (1890), a small Folk Victorian cottage that represents some of the earliest late nineteenth-century development in Westlake.

■ **323 Laveta Ter.** (1908), a property with two very rare remaining examples of Los Angeles "shotgun" houses (both constructed in the same year).

■ **Mackey Apartments,** 1137 S. Cochran Ave. (1939), an International Style multi-family residence in the Wilshire area designed by master architect Rudolph M. Schindler. The apartments were purchased by the Republic of Austria in 1995 and have been renovated by the MAK Center, which offers an artists- and architects-in-residence program at the site.

■ **7205 Beverly Blvd.** (1927), a Moorish style structure that is an early Los Angeles auto service station from the 1920s.

■ **Post-War House/House of Tomorrow,** 4950 Wilshire Blvd. (1946), a Contemporary Ranch/ Mid-Century Modern House commissioned by developer Fritz B. Burns and designed by notable local architects Wurdeman and Becket as a highly publicized model home to

serve as a prototype of post-World War II modern suburban living.

■ **Melrose Avenue Grace Church,** 4014 W. Melrose Ave. (1910), an institutional building in Los Angeles, exhibiting design characteristics of the octagon house model popularized in the nineteenth century by Orson Squire Fowler.

WILSHIRE

■ **6th Street–Orange Street Multi-Family Residential Historic District,** 221 parcels containing two-story, multi-family residences along W. 6th Street and W. Orange Street, between S. San Vicente Boulevard and S. Fairfax Avenue—an intact Period Revival neighborhood built between the 1920s and the 1950s.

■ **DuBarry Apartments,** 3471 W. 5th St. (1929), a French Revival (Norman) apartment building designed by noted movie palace architect S. Charles Lee, and one of several 1920s multi-family buildings in the Wilshire District that featured a distinctive rooftop sign with neon lettering.

■ **Raymond Chandler Residence,** 6520 Drexel Ave. (1926), significant as the home of novelist and screenwriter Raymond Chandler during an important period of his career: 1943 to 1946. During those years, Chandler worked for Paramount Studios and made his debut in screenwriting with screen adaptations of literary works, including James M. Cain's novel, *Double Indemnity.*

BOYLE HEIGHTS

■ **Boyle Heights Presbyterian Church,** 126 N. Chicago St. (1895), a rare 1890s church building in Los Angeles notable for its quality craftsmanship and Queen Anne architecture with Gothic Revival details.

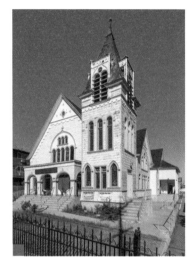 

■ **Kiu Sing Chan Residence,** 2309 E. 3rd St. (1898), a Queen Anne home that is significant as the residence of Kiu Sing Chan, one of the few Chinese Americans to own property in Boyle Heights during a period of anti-immigration sentiment and discrimination against Chinese immigrants. A court interpreter by trade, Chan became the first Methodist minister of Chinese descent in the United States.

■ **Rafu Chuo Gakuen Japanese Language School,** 204 N. Saratoga St., which has provided instruction in Japanese language, conversation, and culture since the 1930s and is one of the few secular Boyle Heights Japanese American institutions to remain in operation.

■ **Casa del Mexicano,** 2900 Calle Pedro Infante, was founded by the Mexican Consulate in 1951 as a cultural center and performance venue for the area's Mexican American population.

BOYLE HEIGHTS

■ **Forsythe Memorial School/Evergreen Hostel,** 506 N. Evergreen Ave. (1914), a Mediterranean Revival structure that was one of several boarding schools operated by the Presbyterian Church with an assimilation-based curriculum, to provide education for girls of Mexican descent in American customs, traditions, and cultural values. The property was reopened as the Evergreen Hostel in 1945, and provided short-term accommodations to Japanese American families returning to Boyle Heights from their internment during World War II. At the time it was photographed in 2020, it was undergoing a significant remodel for future hotel use.

■ **Mexican Mission Church,** 1524 Pleasant Ave. (1930), a Mission Revival church established by celebrity evangelist Aimee Semple McPherson, founder of the Foursquare Church, as one of several small neighborhood churches intended to reach out to the Mexican American community. The church has continuously served a Spanish-speaking population since 1930.

■ **Boyle Avenue Residential Historic District,** a three-block stretch of South Boyle Avenue between 3rd Street and Interstate 5 with twenty-nine properties built between 1887 and 1926, designed in a variety of turn-of-the-century architectural styles including Queen Anne, American Foursquare, and Craftsman; later, multi-family residences were added in several Period Revival styles. The district reflects the early streetcar suburbanization of Boyle Heights and includes the Max Factor Residence at 432 S. Boyle Ave., where the cosmetics executive of Polish-Jewish descent lived from 1923 to 1929. Entrepreneur Andrew A. Boyle was the initial owner of this land; after his death, William H. Workman and John E. Hollenbeck subdivided the acreage, and each constructed large estates near Boyle's residence on the west side of Boyle Avenue.

NORTHEAST LOS ANGELES

■ **1659 W. Colorado Blvd., Eagle Rock** (1919), a building that appears to be the oldest remaining service station structure in the city. Originally constructed on Spring Street in Downtown Los Angeles, it was relocated to its current site in 1931.

■ **Chambers House/Escarpa Pueblo,** 2068 Escarpa Dr., Eagle Rock (1923), a rare local example of Pueblo Revival style residential architecture. Designed by the owner, Virginia Treadwell Chambers, the style incorporates the Hopi symbol for "happiness" in various details and in the floorplan.

■ **Schweizer Verein Helvetia,** 3247 W. Shasta Circle N., Glassell Park (1938), a Swiss Craftsman structure that was the home of the Schweizer Verein Helvetia social club. Originally established in 1887 to bring together the Swiss ethnic population living in Los Angeles, the club congregates to preserve Swiss traditions, assist in assimilation of new immigrants, and foster good relations with its members' new home country.

NORTHEAST LOS ANGELES

■ **Brunswick Avenue Fantasy Bungalows, Atwater Village** (1926–1928), a collection of eighteen single-family residences located on a single block, along the west side of Brunswick Avenue between Appleton Street and Glendale Boulevard. All but one of the residences was built by real estate agent Barney B. Kenoffel, who incorporated Moorish Revival and Egyptian Revival elements into mostly Spanish Colonial Revival residences. Kenoffel drew upon unconventional forms and details inspired by the sets of silent films, including exaggerated piers, decorative parapets, towers, arched openings, and unusual window shapes and patterns.

■ **Florence Crittenton Home,** 234 E. Avenue 33, Glassell Park (1915), significant as the longtime location of a home constructed to provide assistance to young pregnant women. The National Florence Crittenton Mission was founded in New York in the 1890s and expanded to Los Angeles in 1902. This Glassell Park facility, designed in the Mediterranean Revival style, provided these services until 2007, when it was converted to the Los Angeles Leadership Academy.

■ **Lincoln Park Motel,** 2101 Parkside Ave., Lincoln Heights (1929), one of the few remaining examples of a 1920s–1930s motor court in Los Angeles. It was originally the Luna Park Auto Court, constructed by owner-operator Nick Ragenovich on the original Highway 99 route along Mission Road between 1929 and 1931 across from Selig Zoo (later known as Luna Park Zoo and Zoopark), a major Los Angeles tourist attraction that operated between 1915 and 1940.

■ **Holgate Square Residential Historic District,** 2300–2331 Holgate Sq., Lincoln Heights (1911-1925), a small district of nine Spanish Colonial Revival single-family houses in Craftsman and Period Revival styles, with homes arranged around a central square accessed solely from N. Broadway through an entrance marked by tall entry pillars of mortared native cobblestones. The district is significant as an example of streetcar suburbanization in Lincoln Heights and for its elaborate stonework.

■ **310 Mavis Dr., Mount Washington** (1955), a Mid-Century Modern home designed by noted architect Kemper Nomland Jr. as his own residence.

NORTHEAST LOS ANGELES

■ **Paul Sprunck Art Studio and Residence,** 4213 E. Glenmuir Ave., Mount Washington (1922), a Storybook-style residence built in stages between 1922 and 1927 for motion picture artist/art director Paul G. Sprunck.

■ **2419 N. Sichel St., Lincoln Heights** (1887), representing some of the earliest development in Lincoln Heights and an excellent example of Eastlake residential architecture.

■ **Victory Park Bowling Green Viewing Terraces,** Arroyo Seco at Via Marisol and S. A-venue 60, Hermon (1932), a unique masonry terrace complex in Victory Park (now Hermon Park) constructed for the 1932 Olympic Games and one of the few remaining historic resources associated with Los Angeles's first Olympics. The terraces were a viewing area for lawn bowling (though the associated bowling greens have been removed).

■ **Neutra Colony Residential Historic District, Silver Lake,** which consists of ten architect-designed Mid-Century Modern or Late Modern residences concentrated near the intersection of Silver Lake Boulevard and Earl Street, including Neutra Place—a rare concentration of intact residences designed by Richard Neutra and/or his son Dion Neutra, built between 1948 and 1979.

■ **Mabel Normand Feature Film Company,** 1215 N. Bates Ave., Silver Lake (1916), one of Los Angeles's earliest surviving motion picture studios. Normand was a silent film comedienne who occupied the studio in 1916 and 1917; from 1918 to 1921, it housed the production company of cowboy star William S. Hart. The studio now operates as Mack Sennett Studios, named after the man who built it.

■ **Ralph G. Walker House,** 2100 N. Kenilworth Ave., Silver Lake (1936), an International style residence designed by Rudolph Schindler and designated as Historic-Cultural Monument #1161 in 2018.

■ **Orans Residence,** 2404 Micheltorena St., Silver Lake (1941), a distinctive International style residence designed by Gregory Ain.

■ **1536 N. Easterly Ter., Silver Lake** (1936), a Streamline Moderne single-family residence designed by William Kesling, and a highly worthy companion to Kesling's Skinner House next door at 1530 N. Easterly Ter., designated as HCM #856 in 2006.

▨ **Angona Winery,** 1435 N. McDuff St., Echo Park (1898), a Victorian Vernacular Cottage that, according to the Echo Park Historical Society, was the home of Cono and Antonia Angona, whose family made wine here from 1900 to 1910 with grapes from the San Fernando Valley.

■ **Angelus Temple Church Parsonage,** 1801 W. Park Ave., Echo Park (1925), the home of Aimee Semple McPherson, founder of the Foursquare Church, from 1925 to 1944. Located adjacent to Angelus Temple, a National Historic Landmark. McPherson is significant in the history of religion in Los Angeles and a pioneer in the use of radio for evangelism.

■ **Solano Ave. Homes,** 400–700 W. Solano Ave., Solano Canyon, a grouping of small Victorian cottages built between 1890 and 1910, representing early residential development in this neighborhood.

SOUTHEAST LOS ANGELES

■ **626 E. 54th St., South Park**
(1890), a grand Queen Anne residence
exhibiting high-quality craftsmanship.

■ **616 and 620 E. 21st St., Southeast
Los Angeles** (1895), side-by-side
Dutch Colonial Revival residences
that are part of a grouping of four
nineteenth-century Dutch Colonial
Revival homes in this neighborhood.

■ **Goodyear Gardens Historic
District, Southeast Los Angeles/
Florence** (1920), consisting of forty-
nine single-family residences along E.
59th Place, between Avalon Boulevard
and S. San Pedro Street; significant
as a rare example4 of worker housing
built by an industrial manufacturer,
Goodyear Tire & Rubber Company,
which was located nearby on
Central Avenue. Of 550 acres of
land purchased by Goodyear for
industrial development in Southeast
Los Angeles, eighty acres were set
aside for affordable housing to be sold
to Goodyear employees. Goodyear
hired architects Sumner Hunt and
Silas Burns to design homes for the
development. The neighborhood
continued to be largely occupied by
the families of workers in nearby
factories through the mid-twentieth
century.

■ **California Eagle Publishing Company Offices,** 4071 S. Central Ave., Vernon-Central (1906), location of the offices of a newspaper, *The California Eagle*, that is significant for its decades-long role in the Black community.

■ **Holy Redeemer Church** (now St. Lawrence of Brindisi), 10124 S. Compton Ave., Watts (1948), a late Mission Revival style church with a characteristically shaped parapet, tower, and arched entryway; one of the most architecturally significant buildings in Watts.

■ **St. Philip the Evangelist Church,** 2716 S. Stanford Ave., Southeast Los Angeles (1929), significant to the African American community as the earliest African American Episcopal congregation in Los Angeles, founded in 1906.

■ **Mafundi Institute,** 1827 E. 103rd St., Watts (1969), a significant community center created for local artists, writers, musicians, filmmakers and poets in the aftermath of the 1965 Watts uprising, designed by architect Arthur Silvers.

SOUTH LOS ANGELES

■ **1924 W. Rochester Circle, Exposition Park** (1941), the grand Colonial Revival home designed by Paul R. Williams that was the residence of Eddie "Rochester" Anderson, an African American actor and comedian best-known for his long-running role on radio and television in *The Jack Benny Show.*

■ **Hacienda Hotel,** 9141 S. Figueroa St., Vermont Vista (1953), site of the 1964 murder of internationally acclaimed singer Sam Cooke, one of the pioneers of soul music.

■ **Pepperdine College Historic District** on Vermont Avenue between Florence and Manchester, Vermont Knolls, the historic location of Pepperdine University, which opened in 1937 and relocated to Malibu in 1972. The district, which is an enclosed campus oriented around a central landscaped quadrangle, includes four Streamline Moderne buildings designed by John M. Cooper.

■ **Van de Kamp Building,** 4153 S. Figueroa, Exposition Park (1930), one of the few remaining examples within Los Angeles of an original Van de Kamp Bakery building, with its iconic windmill design.

■ **Temple Tifereth Israel,** 1561 W. Martin Luther King Jr. Blvd., Exposition Park (1932), a Romanesque Revival synagogue with high-quality design and craftsmanship. Though now occupied by a Baptist church, the structure retains Hebrew text over the entry and a stained glass window with a Star of David, as well as visual cues relating to the Spanish and Portuguese roots of the Sephardic congregation.

■ **Vermont Knolls Historic District,** a distinct residential neighborhood developed between 1928 and 1939, with 487 parcels bounded by 79th Street, 83rd Street, and Normandie Avenue to the west. Most of Vermont Knolls consists of one-story, single-family houses with striking consistency and regularity of massing, setbacks, lot coverage, and plan, despite a variety of forms and styles.

■ **Ella Fitzgerald Residence,** 3971 S. Hepburn Ave., Baldwin Hills (1949), the home of the renowned jazz singer, who lived in this house from 1957 to 1980, the period in which she recorded the majority of her catalog.

■ **Leimert Theatre,** 3341 W. 43rd Pl., Leimert Park (1931), now known as the Vision Theatre, an Art Deco movie theater that is an artistic anchor of the Leimert Park community.

■ **Fifth Avenue Christian Church,** 1426 S. 5th Ave., West Adams/Jefferson Park (1901), a rare surviving church from this time period and one of the earliest buildings in the neighborhood, with Queen Anne and Gothic Revival influences.

■ **2125 S. 4th Ave., West Adams/ Arlington Heights** (1906), a Craftsman residence with unusual Exotic Revival elements, such as keyhole windows in the main façade.

■ **4245 W. Don Alanis Pl., Baldwin Hills**
(1958), a beautifully sited and executed
Mid-Century Modern residence, and an
early work of noted architect Raymond
Kappe.

■ **The Leimert Park Historic District,**
which includes about 1,200 buildings built
between 1927 and 1945, generally bounded
by 39th Street, Vernon Avenue, Crenshaw
Boulevard, and 3rd Avenue. Developed
by Walter H. Leimert, it represents an
early Los Angeles planned residential
community with buildings in a variety
of styles, including Spanish Colonial
Revival and Streamline Moderne. The
neighborhood later broke through racially
restrictive housing practices to become
home to African American and Japanese
American communities. Leimert Park
Village, the commercial district, emerged
as a significant African American cultural
center beginning in the 1960s.

■ **The Crenshaw Seinan Historic
District,** which includes seventy-one
properties on Crenshaw Boulevard,
Bronson Avenue, and Norton Avenue
between Coliseum and 39th Streets, is
significant for its association with the
Japanese American community that
settled here in the years following World
War II. The neighborhood features visual
characteristics and landscaping evocative
of Japanese design traditions.

SAN PEDRO

■ **Atchinson House,** 1192 W. 17th St. (1907), a Queen Anne home with Carpenter Gothic influences, built by Captain Mitchell "Mike" Duffy, who owned and operated the first harbor ferry service in San Pedro.

■ **Norwegian Methodist Episcopal Church,** 238 N. Mesa St. (1902), a Gothic Revival church that was an early building associated with the Norwegian community, which historically resided in San Pedro; it now hosts a Spanish-speaking congregation. The church pre-dates San Pedro's consolidation with the City of Los Angeles in 1909.

■ **Peck Park,** 560 N. Western Ave. (1929), one of four parks developed in the 1920s and 1930s on lands donated by early city pioneer and developer George Huntington Peck Jr., who named the other three parks (Leland Park, Alma Park, and Rena Park) after his children. These parks were developed to promote San Pedro as a livable "city of homes" and include mature trees, decorative plantings, pedestrian pathways, and foot bridges, as well as bandstands and amphitheaters.

■ **Dalmatian-American Club of San Pedro,** 1639 S. Palos Verdes St. (1935), a social club associated with the Croatian community, founded in 1926; the club constructed a new headquarters in the Art Deco style in 1935.

■ **Fitzsimmons Market/Garden Basket No. 2,** 1231 S. Pacific Ave. (1935), a rare remaining 1930s neighborhood market that was associated with the Japanese American community that historically resided in San Pedro, as well as the local Norwegian community. The building became San Pedro Ballet School in 1988.

■ **1100 S. Dodson Ave.** (1932), a residence that exhibits the significant features of American Colonial Revival architecture, including fixed wood shutters and classical balustrades.

■ **Storybook Homes,** 1167 and 1175 W. 10th St. (1925), an unusual side-by-side pairing of two homes in the Storybook/Tudor Revival style.

WILMINGTON ✕ HARBOR CITY

■ **Granada Theatre,** 632 N. Avalon Blvd., Wilmington (1925), a neighborhood theater with Renaissance Revival architectural influences.

■ **Don Hotel,** 906 N. Avalon Blvd., Wilmington (1929), the most prestigious hotel in Wilmington during the pre-World War II period, constructed to cater to tourists going to and from Catalina Island, with a classic rooftop sign oriented to catch the attention of motorists traveling north.

■ **712 E. O St., Wilmington** (1890), a small Victorian Vernacular hipped-roof cottage that appears to be one of the oldest residences in the area, from the period prior to Wilmington's consolidation with the City of Los Angeles.

◼ **Arturo's Fine Mexican Food,** 25720 S. Western Ave., Harbor City (1960), an exceptionally intact Mid-Century Modern restaurant with original signage, lighting, and landscaping. Arturo's served as a community gathering place in Harbor City from 1960 to 2014, and is now named Miches de la Baja.

◼ **International Longshore and Warehouse Union-Pacific Maritime Association (ILWU-PMA) Training Center,** 639 N. Fries Ave., Wilmington (1963), a union hall that reflects the important role of labor unions and the port in the history of Wilmington.

◼ **Olympic Ice Arena,** 23770 S. Western Ave., Harbor City (1962), a Mid-Century Modern ice skating rink that played a significant role in the recreational life of harbor communities.

■ **Tepper Tire Service Station,** 762 W. Gardena Blvd. (1922), a rare surviving 1920s service station, which is likely one of the oldest largely intact examples of this property type in the entire city.

■ **The Yamada Company,** 700 W. Gardena Blvd. (1956), a building significant as the location of one of the oldest remaining Japanese American businesses in the greater Gardena area; the company moved to this location from Downtown Los Angeles in 1956.

■ **Pacific Telephone/AT&T Building,** 17200 S. Vermont Ave. (1970), a building constructed for Pacific Telephone to house equipment, designed in the Late Modern style by architect C. Day Woodford.

■ **Chacksfield Tract Residential Historic District,** north of the Gardena Freeway (SR 91), south of W. 168th Street, east of Vermont Avenue, and west of the Harbor Freeway (I-110); comprised of two tracts developed in 1956 and 1957 by George E. Chacksfield Homes Inc., and in 1961 by the Grand Land Company. The neighborhood retains a strong sense of time and place, and is characterized by Japanese-style gardens, reflecting the changing demographics of the area in the postwar era.

HARBOR GATEWAY

■ **Alondra Palms,** Alondra Boulevard between Menlo Ave. and Ainsworth St., a notable grouping of mature Mexican Fan Palms dating from the earliest development of the community in 1905.

■ **Roosevelt Memorial Park Organ Pavilion Building,** 18255 S. Vermont Ave. (1925), a freestanding building designed to house a Wurlitzer pipe organ that has been called "The Mightiest Wurlitzer" because it was designed to project music throughout the vast cemetery grounds; it was said to be audible from five miles away. While the building remains intact, the organ was damaged by the 1933 Long Beach earthquake and became unplayable by 1959; it was removed and remains in storage today.

■ **519 W. 121st St.** (1912), a Craftsman-style residence that is one of only a few Craftsman homes in the Harbor Gateway community.

ACKNOWLEDGMENTS

Because *Preserving Los Angeles* features the work of the City of Los Angeles historic preservation program over more than a decade, these acknowledgments must reflect not only the mechanics of assembling the book itself, but also those who helped make the featured accomplishments possible.

It truly takes a village to complete a citywide historic resources survey in a city the size of Los Angeles. Over 300 professionals and volunteers contributed to SurveyLA over its ten years, and we can't possibly recognize all of them individually here. Particular thanks must go to Kathryn Welch Howe, who worked for several years on behalf of the Getty Conservation Institute, laying the groundwork for what became SurveyLA. The staff of the Getty Conservation Institute were instrumental to the success of the survey—particularly Tim Whalen, Kathleen Gaines, Jeanne Marie Teutonico, Alison Dalgity, David Myers, and Annabel Enriquez—as was the support of the Getty Foundation, under the leadership of the late Deborah Marrow.

The California State Office of Historic Preservation staff supported the city's annual grant applications, making possible most of the community engagement and cutting-edge work on ethnic/cultural themes.

Much of the research and written content that became the basis for the SurveyLA field guide at the end of this book was generated through the collaborative work of the region's professional historic preservation consulting firms. The Architectural Resources Group (ARG), Galvin Preservation Associates (GPA), and the Historic Resources Group (HRG) took on the bulk of the field surveys, enlightening our Office of Historic Resources (OHR) staff along the way on the best lunch options in every community. SurveyLA also benefited enormously from the contributions of other firms including Chattel Inc., ICF International, LSA Associates, Page & Turnbull, and Sapphos Environmental.

SurveyLA's dedicated Speakers Bureau volunteers served as our emissaries at community meetings and events around Los Angeles, and more than forty office interns contributed to our research and work. More than twenty other historians and architectural historians served as volunteer researchers and authors for the Citywide Historic Context that served as the framework for SurveyLA.

I have been tremendously privileged to work at the OHR alongside the most committed and talented staff team of preservation professionals imaginable.

SurveyLA is a testament to the ingenuity and project management skills of Janet Hansen, who also offered insightful comments on this book's draft manuscript. Lambert Giessinger, our staff architect, has been the backbone of the OHR since day one, consistently finding creative design solutions to preserve and reuse L.A.'s signature historic buildings. And our Historic Preservation Overlay Zone (HPOZ) staff members, past and present—together with more than 200 volunteer HPOZ board members during my tenure—have brought historic preservation into L.A.'s neighborhoods, guiding property owners in making the small, incremental decisions that add up to successful preservation outcomes.

The often-unsung assistance of our L.A. City Planning information technology/systems staff, and particularly Fae Tsukamoto and David Dieudonne, facilitated the development of the customized technology that made SurveyLA possible, supported by consultants at NorthSouth GIS and CPS, Inc.

L.A. City Planning's executive leadership has consistently supported our preservation program, starting with Gail Goldberg, who brought me into the department in 2006, to current Director of Planning Vince Bertoni, who offered his immediate and enthusiastic support when I proposed this book.

Our city Cultural Heritage commissioners during my tenure—Richard Barron, Gail Kennard, Barry Milofsky, Pilar Buelna, Diane Kanner, Elissa Scrafano, Jeremy Irvine, Carlos Singer, Stanley Stalford Jr., Alma Carlisle, Mia Lehrer, Glen Dake, Roella Louie, Oz Scott, Tara Jones Hamacher, and Mary Klaus Martin—have consistently pushed and supported our staff while making thoughtful judgment calls on nominations of Historic-Cultural Monuments, such as those described in Chapter 1.

A CITY AT PRESERVATION'S LEADING EDGE: THE LOS ANGELES BASIN AND DOWNTOWN FROM THE GRIFFITH OBSERVATORY

I will always be grateful to former Los Angeles City Councilmember and City Controller Laura Chick, and the close-knit staff "family" she built, for giving me my first full-time urban planning opportunity in city government, and for consistently demonstrating the power of candor, integrity, and independent leadership in government.

I owe my historic preservation career to Linda Dishman, who lured me out of the city council office to join the Los Angeles Conservancy and gave me an unparalleled master class in the art of historic preservation. Linda and all of my former colleagues and more recent successors at the Conservancy have created a vibrant preservation constituency that has created and sustained Los Angeles's municipal preservation program.

The featured photos could not have been accomplished, especially during a period of COVID-19 social

All Angelenos owe Paddy Calistro and Scott McAuley their gratitude for making Angel City Press such a welcoming home for authors who have compellingly interpreted Los Angeles, in all its facets and complexity, over nearly three decades. Thanks to ACP's Terri Accomazzo for her keen editing eye, to Kate Murray for her skillful proofreading, and to Amy Inouye, whose book designs are never anything short of eye-catching. Kate Whitney-Schubb was a godsend to our project as an intern/researcher, keeping our photo research, acquisition, and management well-organized.

The interest and support of my family members—including my siblings, Karen and Lee, and my Uncle Jerry—helped convince me that there might be wider interest in our preservation work. I will always be tremendously grateful for the boundless love and pride of my mom as well as my dad, who avidly followed my office's e-newsletters highlighting L.A.'s historic places before he passed away.

My children (who've suddenly become young adults), Daniel and Emily, keep me grounded and connected to emerging realities, always with their unique spirit and humor. They've also long indulged my penchant to turn family trips into impromptu explorations of "downtown historic cores"—even when Emily often felt compelled to grumble, "Oh, no: another historic plaque!"

And above all, I owe *Preserving Los Angeles* to my remarkable wife, Kathy, who prodded me for years to write this book, and then turned her skillful editor's pen to all of my first drafts. Kathy has been my sounding board ever since we met as college undergraduates, though she never imagined that, through osmosis, planning and preservation lingo such as "CEQA" or "adaptive reuse" would someday fall trippingly from her tongue.

distancing, without the assistance of many building owners and representatives: Stefano Curti and Giuseppina Buonfantino (Biscuit Company Lofts), Jody Hummer (Hong Office Building), Jim Poulos (Pann's), Kathryn Gillan (Vibiana), Mark Thaler (Bullocks Wilshire/Southwestern Law School), Doug Lynn (Wilshire Boulevard Temple), Brandon Patterson (Eastern Columbia), Diana Wright (Hollywood Sign), Melanie Hawkins-Robertson (28th Street Apartments), Joan Maltese (CDI Learning Center), and Reverend Rhodell Glasco (New Temple Missionary Baptist Church). Christina Rice of the L.A. Public Library also provided invaluable help on historic images. Since no cameras or photos are typically allowed inside its gates, the photos of the Garden of Oz, permitted through the generosity of Gail Cottman, offer an exclusive look at one of Los Angeles's most unique and hidden historic landmarks.

SITE INDEX

ABOUT THE AUTHORS

KEN BERNSTEIN has devoted much of his career to preserving and enhancing the unique architecture and cultural heritage of America's second-largest city, using historic preservation to transform communities. For Los Angeles City Planning, he  directs the Office of Historic Resources and Urban Design Studio and has directed the department's citywide planning and community planning initiatives. He has led the creation of Los Angeles' comprehensive historic preservation program and the completion of SurveyLA, a ground-breaking citywide survey of L.A.'s historic resources. He previously directed the preservation advocacy work of the Los Angeles Conservancy, the nation's largest local preservation organization.

 STEPHEN SCHAFER is a photographer with a preservation distraction. His 33-year career behind a camera spans all aspects of commercial photography and he now specializes on both new and historic architecture. In 1996 he and his wife Sherry began a seemingly endless rehabilitation of a shaky little 1881 folk Victorian Farmhouse, it was during this project that he was afflicted with the "preservation bug," which he probably contracted from a stray redwood splinter. Ever since, he has been drawn to vintage buildings great and small. He now crisscrosses America documenting significant places for the National Register of Historic Places and the Historic American Buildings Survey collection at the Library of Congress.

PANN'S RESTAURANT, 6710 LA TIJERA BLVD., WESTCHESTER

PHOTO CREDITS

The images in *Preserving Los Angeles* are the copyrighted work of architectural photographer Stephen Schafer except as noted below.

David Abel, 145
Helena Arahuete, 167
Anna Aran, via Flickr/Creative Commons, 44
Shari Belafonte, 144
Ken Bernstein, 28, 44, 190
Brookfield Properties, 119
California State Library, 139
Canter's Deli, 97
Chattel, Inc., 101, 140, 141
Amy Dickerson, 70
Federal Aviation Administration, 150
Getty Research Institute, Julius Shulman Photographs, © J. Paul Getty Trust, Los Angeles, 16, 18, 24, 32
Bobby Green, 27, photograph by Maiko Naito; 39
Greg Headley, 201
Alan Hess, 179
HistoricPlacesLA, Office of Historic Resources, 100, 166, 171, 199
Brent Huss, 42
KFA Architecture, 121
Koning Eizenberg Architecture, 134, 135
Larchmont Buzz, 63

Library of Congress: Historic American Engineering Record Repository, 46; Prints & Photographs Division, HAER-CA-271-30, Brian Grogan Photographer, 2001, 47
LockeMichael Michael Locke, 99
Los Angeles City Planning's Office of Historic Resources, 81, 83
Los Angeles Department of Transportation, 161
Los Angeles Public Library Photo Collection: Bob Baker Marionette Theater Collection, 25; Los Angeles Herald Examiner Collection, 37; Shades of L.A. Collection, 95; Security Pacific National Bank Photo Collection, 125, 148
Los Angeles Times, 36, 80
William Malouf, 34
Metro Library and Archive, 118
Barry Milofsky, 29
Sarah Ohta, 103
Omgiving, 117
Richard Nixon Presidential Library and Museum, 33
Merrill H. Scott Family, 52
Steve Sherman Photography, 255
University of Southern California Libraries: ONE Archives, 51, 92, 99; California Historical Society Collection, 113
Photo by Neal Vickers, licensed under the Creative Commons Attribution-Share Alike 4.0 International license, 58
Google Images by Connie Zhou, 151

Preserving Los Angeles: How Historic Places Can Transform America's Cities
By Ken Bernstein
Photography by Stephen Schafer

Copyright © 2021 Kenneth Bernstein and Stephen Schafer

Design by Amy Inouye, Future Studio Los Angeles

10 9 8 7 6 5 4 3 2 1

ISBN-13 978-1-62640-075-7